Breathing Alive

A Guide to Conscious Living

Reshad Feild's spiritual search has taken him around the world to Zen monasteries in Japan, the Himalayas and to Turkey where he studied the Sufi mystical traditions and was initiated into the order of the Mevlevi Dervishes.

He has been in turn a popular singer, an antique dealer and stockbroker. Throughout the 70's he ran schools in human transformation in Britain, Canada and America. A professional geomancer, Reshad was granted his doctorate in psychological counselling in 1983. He is the author of several other books which have been described as classics of contemporary spiritual literature.

By the same author

The Last Barrier
The Invisible Way
Steps to Freedom
Here to Heal
A Travelling People's Feild Guide
Footprints in the Sand

BREATHING ALIVE

A Guide to Conscious Living

Reshad Feild

ELEMENT BOOKS

First published in 1988 by
Element Books Limited
Longmead, Shaftesbury, Dorset

Printed and bound in Great Britain

Designed by Clarke Williams

Cover design by Max Fairbrother
Cover photo : Frank Whitney/Image Bank

British Library Cataloguing in Publication Data

Feild, Reshad
Breathing alive : a guide to conscious Living
1. Self-realisation
I. Title
158'.1

ISBN 1 - 85230 - 050 - 7

This book is dedicated to
all those on the Road of
Truth
and to the seekers
who are looking for it.

Contents

PROLOGUE

*'Just picking up a book does not mean to say
you are going to learn anything.'*

I hope and pray that I will be able to finish this book
before I die!

What a way to start a book about the Art and Science
of Breath, and yet, sitting here, listening to beautiful
music, the first sentence itself becomes almost like a
living prayer. We come into this world on the Breath
of His Compassion, and we go out on the Breath of His
Mercy. In between those two breaths we hold the universe
in our arms in what is called our 'Life-span'. How little we
are awake to this wonder; how seldom we are awake to
the present moment. Yet it *is* possible to wake up to our
responsibility in being born man and woman, and to be
custodians to that which gives us life. God is the Only
Provider, and it is His Mercy and His Compassion, but we
are His witnesses. The universe is made for us; it is given
to us in this theatre of life in which we play out our roles
and functions, responding as consciously as we can to
the direct needs of the moment itself.

So often we merely drift around, tossed and turned
by the hazards of fate, not putting ourselves in the stream
of service, and therefore into the arms of destiny. We
presume life; we presume the breath. We presume that we
will wake up tomorrow, or that we are conscious human
beings, without making any real effort to pay for the very
life that we have been given. And so we are frightened of
death. We are frightened of facing the Great Unknown.
We do not see that this life is the only one we have, and
therefore the greatest adventure in the world! We cannot
know what will come after this life as long as we merely
live in the illusion of our own separation. In separation
we cannot know what will come after this brief life-span
of ours. We can presume, and we can make up all sorts

of dreams and fantasies. But we do not know, and that is what makes this life such a total adventure! Today is the only day that we have, and the only day that we can truly have dominion over ourselves. We would be foolish indeed if we were to waste this day. We are foolish if we waste even one single breath. It is said that wastage is the only sin, and sin is a lack of knowledge.

Breath is Life, and *the Life* can never die. Without breath we pass into clouds of fantasy, waiting for the wind to change so that we can find ourselves once again, find our true heritage which is true freedom. God does not want us to be bound by chains of illusion. He does not want us to face the wall of the cave, when we have only to turn round, once again, and see the Light that was always there from the beginning of time. The God within is imprisoned by the degree of our resentment, envy and pride, the walls that divide us from Truth. God is within, waiting to be released through the knowledge that indeed we are loved. And God is Love! It is we who have to wake up and thus free the imprisoned God. It is we who need to know that Breath is Life.

What is this breath that is talked about so often? Actually it is not so difficult to understand when we come to realise that on planet Earth we have just one thing in common and that is the element of air. We sit in a room attending a lecture or concert; we are all sharing the same air. We may not consider this important, and yet, the moment we enter a world of compassion, knowing that the musicians and the conductor in the concert, or he who is giving the lecture, are all sharing the same air with us, something can happen within to help bring about real change.

We come into this world on the breath and we go out of this world on the breath. We share the same air. Now what a challenge that is! What happens to the air from the moment it enters our body on the in-breath and the time in the relative world that it takes for the breath to go out into a waiting world? What does happen? Can real change come about if we are not awake to the beauty of the moment? Perhaps if we are asleep, the air that we have breathed in will go out from us in a poor state, rather than having been used consciously in the necessary process of transformation. Yet we are transformers of subtle energies. It is part of our life's work and obligation in gratefulness to the One Source of All Life. Could it be possible that with the breath we could fill up our own universe with loving kindness, beauty and well-being? We could open our arms, encompassing our universe, receive the bounty that is always here, and then transform all that is necessary to breathe out hope to a world that surely needs it. Knowledge anchors Love, and it is the knowledge of ourselves that ultimately releases, in the joy of recognition, the pure energy that gives life to the planet. The breath of the mystic turns the world.

This book is written from the heart and, in a sense, brings into completion the other books that I have written over the years. There is nothing new in what I teach and speak about. The book carries ideas from the world of ideas; it carries possibilities from the world of possibility. It carries hope from its own world, and it carries well-tempered steel of the sword of Truth for those who will not be kind to themselves and others. It does not placate people's self-righteousness. Again, as in my previous books, it puts the onus of responsibility right back onto the individual. We can be taught about the sacredness of breath and of life itself. We can even be taught how to breathe, the rhythm, beauty and the wonder of it all, but we have to do it ourselves.

I pray that this book will be one which can be read by anyone – not just by those who feel that they are treading 'the Spiritual Path'. There is such a great danger that we can feel special in some way, rather than realising that finding ourselves is the most normal thing of all! The spiritual path is not separate from everyday life. Far from it! When we feel special, then we forget to breathe consciously. We don't have to be seen as saints, prophets or masters. There have been enough in this last epoch to act as examples to us all. To be normal is indeed a very great challenge. Imagine what a breath of relief it will be when we actually *know* we are normal! We are balanced.

Our in-breath and our out-breath are balanced. We love as we know we are loved. The womb of the moment, lying within the pause between the two breaths of life and death, is a world of infinite possibility, waiting to give birth to a new cycle of Mankind – the Golden Age that we have heard about for so long.

Reshad Feild

1

SHELLS ON THE SAND

*'The greatest healing in the world
is being yourselves.'*

We walked along the beach. It's a favourite place for us.
The sand stretches out two or three miles in a great curve.
Hardly anyone goes there for it would mean walking from
where you park the car, and people don't like walking
much in the States. In fact, there is not even a car park
and so the herd instinct doesn't come into play. People
do so love to cluster into herds, partly for self-protection
and partly from fear of the unknown.

The beach is near Santa Cruz, not far away actually.
Perhaps you will find it one day. Just look for a clump of
trees way out there towards the water, going north, and
a small gate, with enough room for two or three cars to
park in front of it. A path will lead you through the wide
meadow and past the eucalyptus grove to our favourite
spot. Once we lay down in a gully on top of a bed of wild
strawberries. Somehow, in the beauty of the moment, I
had not noticed that one of the lenses of my glasses
had fallen out on the walk from the car. The chances
of finding the lense again were seemingly impossible, but
we asked and asked the inner guide to help us and we
did find it hundreds of yards away lying in the tall grass.
Could it have been the knowledge in the breath that led
us to the right place?

On the beach, if you are very awake, you can find
abalone shells, those hand-sized mother-of-pearl shells
that are the prize of collectors all over the world. They
are washed up on the high tide and then get hidden in the
sand, sometimes with just a little of the shell sticking up

into the air, reflecting the light of the sun. But you have to be in the right frame of mind, the right attitude, to find them. If you are not awake, collected in all of your being and on top of the breath, you will miss them. You can walk right over them and never notice their beauty. You can walk those two or three miles day after day and you will not find the abalone shells.

On the other hand, if you are awake to all the beauty of God's creatures and in love with the world and His creation you may suddenly find yourself attuned in a very special way and the shells will show themselves to you. Once you have found one, then quite suddenly you can find them everywhere. When you are in love on the beach, you will find the shells. It is the same throughout our lives. When we are in love with life itself, all manner of strange and beautiful things happen to us and we discover, finally, that we are being guided home.

I remember one day when we were there we saw a little old lady with a sack over her shoulder. She, too, was looking for the same shells. She was looking so hard, so very hard, and yet she had only found one broken piece of shell. We greeted her and smiled in recognition.

Sitting down on the sand, we looked out over the Pacific ocean and watched the tide come in over the little pools that hide all those miraculous creatures, shrimp, sea urchins, tiny coloured fish and beautiful sea plants that wave the tide in and out. The old lady passed us by, barely looking up from her search. We waved. She did not seem to find anything. A while later she came back along the sand once more. Her sack was empty. She held the piece of shell she had found in her hand. Maybe that day she was not awake.

We watched her climb back over the rocks and up towards the long path to the road. Just then, as our breath danced in the wind, Nur cried out, 'Look. Just over there!' pointing her finger towards what she was seeing. She got up and there, not a hundred feet in front of us, was a flash of iridescent colour bursting up from the sand. An abalone shell! The old lady must have walked right over it. Nur took it, so carefully, from the sand and then ran down to the water, washed the sand away and brought it back to me. It was a perfect red shell. There are several types but for me the small red abalone, unchipped and shining in its purity, is the most beautiful of them all. I held it in my hands, wondering at the beauty of God's creation once again. I never know whether it is His Beauty that brings us to fall in love or whether it is the recognition of His Beauty that brings Love to life. Perhaps it is both. I do know that whenever we recognise God's beauty in His creation then someone else will also find it in their own lives and fall in love themselves.

There is a story I always remember about bringing life to the world. Many years ago I was living in a motel in Los Angeles, just near to the freeway. It was in the early days of the so-called 'spiritual movement'. Gurus were springing up like flowers in the desert after the first rains. The word 'meditation' was seen as a visiting card to enlightenment, or so some people thought, and yet there were many casualties on the road. We used to call them 'the walking wounded of the spiritual path'.

One morning a group of people who had come to my lecture and seminar, offered to take a friend and myself to a little park near Hollywood. Unfortunately few who attend workshops week after week learn very much. There are always so many different choices out there in the spiritual supermarket, and so it almost forces people to live in a world of comparison which feeds the mind and seldom satisfies the heart. On the walk we were discussing how most people are totally asleep to the Breath of Life, and yet it is true that without conscious breathing we are only partially alive, and therefore our understanding must indeed be limited.

I am sure that we were talking too much, and listening too little, for, quite suddenly, we were given a shock which woke everyone up. We were walking along a path. There was only one tree in that area. Just as we got close to it a little bird fell dead off a branch in front of us on the path. I had never seen anything like that happen before. We all stopped in our tracks, silent and awestruck. The bird lay there in the dust, not a flicker of movement coming from its body. I remember it was a grey-green colour. In that shock and in that moment of silence, you could almost hear everyone taking a conscious breath. It often happens that way, when a miraculous moment is given to us and we are taken out of time and space as we normally know it. For some, that conscious breath is taken only on their death bed.

Then came one of those unforgettable moments that will always remain with me. My friend walked quietly forwards towards the dead bird. Turning to the others, I indicated that they should remain still and silent. It was as though the whole universe and the complete cycle of history was in those few steps that she took. Bending down, she picked up the bird in her hands and brought it to her breast. Its little eyes were closed and its tiny claws were clenched up towards the sky. We watched her as she came into the Breath, the Breath of Life, and then she lifted up the bird and blew quietly into it. I don't know what I saw first, whether it was the bird's eyes opening or the unclenching of the little feet. Still lying on its back in her hands, the bird started to move its head from side to side, looking around. It had come to life again. Perhaps it was seeing the world for the first time. My friend raised up her arms. We watched the bird gaining confidence with every second. And then it turned over, looked around once more, and flew away across the gully by the edge of the path. We did not say anything. There was no explanation. We walked silently on to complete our walk.

2

A Thin Rope of Air

*'We want to love people but usually only in
the condition we want them to be. If we're
not awake to the one thing that we share in
common, which is air, then how can we love
each other unconditionally?'*

There is a wonderful saying from the Sufi Tradition: 'Hold
fast to the rope of God'. Like so many of these sayings,
we are given them as a challenge. The meaning is not
explained by the teacher but rather we are left holding the
question in our hearts.

What is this 'Rope of God'? Do we have one tailor-
made for each of us or is it like the fakir's magic rope
which uncurls upwards and then provides something
for him to climb up before disappearing into thin air? Or
could it just be that the secret is something to do with the
element of air itself?

So many times we are told that we must remember
ourselves and finally know ourselves. We are told to love
the Lord our God and to love our neighbour as ourself.
But how often are we reminded that we are sharing the
same air? If only every little child, from kindergarten on,
would be taught this at the beginning of every class, it
would surely make for a better world. After all, we come
into the world on the breath and we go out on the breath.
It is what we do with the air that counts.

Let me explain it this way. Water is a conductor
of electricity. We all know this. It is not the very best
conductor but it surely is a conductor. A thought-form
is an electrical impulse. All of us are composed of over
80 per cent water. That is a scientific fact. This water,

as a conductor, draws thought to itself and so we can be seen to be full of thought, imprisoned in a cage, wanting to be freed, to be redeemed back to the Source, for all time and for all people. A thought-form needs a human being through which it can manifest itself. It can't really manage to manifest itself through a horse or a dog. An instinctual portion of it can but that is all. It needs us poor human beings to grab onto. Right?

Breath also contains moisture. Every little droplet of moisture on the breath can contain loving thoughts; or it can contain negativity, producing with it an atmosphere which is surely not going to give pleasure and joy to the world. The moisture can collect floating thought-forms in the same way that we can get hay fever from the pollen of grasses and flowers that we are allergic to. We need to get our water systems organised – i.e. that 80 per cent of us which is mainly a thought-collector. With conscious use of the breath we can combine the elements of fire, earth, air and water into an alchemical marriage to distil the thought-forms that are no longer necessary in the world.

Let's really look at it. Breath is Life. The Life itself can never die. The Life itself is Everlasting Life. Breath is not limited by walls or concrete floors, nor is it limited by time as we know it. I look out of the window as I am typing this chapter and I breathe out love into the world. I know that someone, somewhere or other, in this time or another time, will wake up to know that they are loved.

Is this not a great challenge? Can we see the responsibility we have in being born man and woman and in learning how to breathe consciously? Let's go back to the first principles once again. We enter a room. We greet our friends. Perhaps we shake hands. Already there is a connection, an association is made on some level or other. Yet how many people take one conscious breath? How many of us remember that, in loving respect for each other, we are sharing the same air? Could you imagine what a difference it would make to a political meeting if this was remembered? The whole world could change.

It is all so simple really. We are unique individuals and each individual is uniquely beautiful. It could not be otherwise since God made us in His Image and God is beautiful. When we know that we are loved then there is no separation between ourselves and the Source of all Life, Everlasting Life, and the Breath goes on for ever. It is then not only our breath, but it is the Breath of God in His Compassion for the world. As it is said, 'I was a hidden treasure and I loved to be known so I created the world that I might be known.' (Hadith of the Prophet)

The rope of God is entwined around our necks. God never wanted to be separated from us so He put this noose around that sacred part of us. He put our head on top of our shoulders and gave us a throat centre from which to speak, a gullet through which we take our food and a tube through which the breath goes to give us life. He gave us an Adam's apple which bobs up and down when we swallow and told us that he would give us food and water, that we could best serve and be conscious custodians of the planet itself. A pretty clever friend this God of ours. If He had not given us a neck and a throat and a passage for the beautiful element of air, we just wouldn't be alive and that would be a waste of God's time and ours, if you see what I mean!

We are being continuously hauled through a hole in space and time, by this thin rope of air, until we can surrender and know, once and for all, that we are loved. 'Die before ye die,' it is said in the Sufi Tradition, and above all the ancient Greek mystery temples were written the words, 'Abandon hope all ye who enter here'. We don't need hope anymore as we are pulled through the walls of illusion by Truth, for Truth and in Truth itself. We are given the Breath of Life. We are given Life itself and now we are asked to learn how to breathe consciously for the sake of our Creator, for our children and our children's children. We are the custodians of the planet.

3

ONCE UPON A TIME

*'Hū means that which is beyond all form. It also
means the carrying force or energy, from one
world to another, from the world of possibility
to the world of manifestation. It is not forcing
the sound. It is reflecting, as in the sound in a
mirror, what you hear when you hear the sound
of the wind in the trees.'*

'Once upon a time . . .' – all good fairy stories start with
these words. I wonder if we have ever considered what
they actually mean. 'Once upon a time' means to stand
on top of time. When we stand on top of time we have
conquered the illusion of life and death. We stand in the
arms of Destiny rather than controlled by the hands of
Fate.

When we are breathing consciously, we are truly
alive. There is freedom and a special sound can be
heard. If you stop and listen very carefully you can
hear it everywhere. It is the sound that the wind makes
blowing through the trees. It is the sound that you hear
in the electrical circuits of your house. I can hear it
coming from the washing machine and I can hear it
sing in the hearts of all children. I can hear it in my
brothers and sisters, although, after so much pain and
suffering, it can be covered up and stifled in disillusion-
ment.

Listen to it now. It is the sound of *Hū*. It is an Arabic
word. Really it is not translatable for it carries all language
within its voice. In the *Hū* there can be no division. There
can only be the real understanding of brotherhood. When
you turn to your friend, greeting the God within them,

and hear the sound of $H\bar{u}$ at the same time, you free the imprisoned God who has been there a long, long time waiting to be recognised.

Once upon a time a man lived by himself on the beach. He had built a wooden hut, just above the high-tide mark. His house was protected from the wind by a stockade of driftwood he had collected. Inside the stockade was a most beautiful garden. Flowers grew where flowers did not normally grow. Young trees peeped out above the fence. There was even a little pond with a simple bench beside it.

Nobody knew how long he had lived there but the people in the village said that he arrived one night many years ago. They couldn't quite remember when. He was different from everyone else they said, although he did his shopping locally and went to the village barber-shop to have his beard trimmed once a week. Otherwise the old man didn't leave his house or go to the pub to talk with the local people. He didn't even have a television. Thus he was definitely thought to be odd.

Some of the villagers were frightened of him and because of that only a few of the children dared to go near the hut where he lived. They came back with stories of strange sounds coming from inside. The grown-ups were worried and asked the children what they heard. 'Well,' ventured one little girl, 'there were sounds like the wind in the pine trees and sometimes the breaking of surf on the beach on a calm night.' A little boy said that it wasn't like that at all but the sounds reminded him of the cracking of thunder on a spring day. The little girl even admitted to having gone down to the beach on her own and she swore that she had seen the old man draw strange symbols in the sand, just below the high-tide mark. When she went back again the tide had come up and they were all gone. 'What's more,' she said, 'some of my friends went down to the beach one night and they saw the old man sitting on the beach, facing the moon. They said that he seemed to be moving in a funny sort of way and that he was singing in another language. It wasn't English anyway . . .' The grown-ups muttered amongst themselves and mutually

decided that the old man was undoubtedly mad but
harmless.

One day, as spring was moving into summer, a young
man walked into the village. He was smartly dressed, with
his suit and tie, and the villagers guessed that he must
have come from one of the big cities. He walked straight
into the post office and said, 'I have heard that there is an
old man who lives not far from here on the sea-shore. Will
you please direct me to him?'

Those who were in the post office rallied together.
One of the older men raised his stick at the young man.
'You don't want to bother with him sir,' he said. 'He's
quite mad, makes strange sounds and sits and watches the
moon. He's caused quite enough trouble in this village.
Now you go away and leave us alone . . .'.

The postmistress was grumpy but she was also inter-
ested. Eventually she said that she would get someone to
show him the way and told him that no one was responsible but himself. She fluffed up her skirts, went outside
and found the little girl who had given the information
about the signs outside the hut. 'You go there with him,'
she said. 'But hasten on home.'

The young man touched the brim of his hat, smiling
gratefully, and set off, following the girl along the path to
the beach. When they reached the end of the path she
turned and left him. He went on alone.

For the next three days the village went on about its
business. It wasn't long before the meeting with the city
gent was forgotten, at least by most of the villagers, but
there were one or two who were wondering just what *did*
happen to him when he left those three days ago. They
decided to see the postmistress and ask her advice.

'Oh my goodness,' she said. 'I had almost forgotten.
I expect he's gone back. It's just like city people. They
seem to think they can come and go as they please.
Anyway it is as likely as not that he got frightened and
never got to the hut. Now don't you worry,' she said,
shooing them out of the office. 'It will be all right.'

But people became inquisitive, as people do. One
evening a few of the men met in the pub just after it

opened. They sat on the benches gazing out over the sand dunes and, after several glasses of ale and pipes of tobacco, they agreed that they had better be responsible and see if they could find out what had happened to the young man. After all, the old man had not been to the village shop for over a week, nor had he had his beard trimmed.

As the sun was setting they walked quietly down the little path towards the beach. There were long shadows lying over the sand dunes. The breakers were quiet in the evening light. The hut wasn't far away. One by one, trying to make no noise, they climbed carefully to the top of the dunes. And there they were! There they both were indeed, the young man and the old man, sitting in front of the hut with their backs turned to face the setting sun.

The villagers looked at one another. They could hear the sound of the wind in the pine trees and yet there were no pine trees on the beach. There was not a breath of wind on the surface of the ocean. The sound seemed to be coming from the two men by the hut. Their bodies were moving rhythmically. All around them there seemed to be a strange peace and a light that spread out across the sand. One by one the people quickly turned around and hastened back towards the village. There was a long discussion in the pub that night!

The next evening the villagers went back – more of them this time. They climbed to the top of the dunes and peeped over. It was the same! This time they watched for a long while, and then, as the last rays of the sun dropped over the sea and the emerald light shone for a moment, the old man and the young man got up. It wasn't difficult to notice the dozen or so villagers sitting on top of the dunes. 'Come and join us,' they said. 'Come on. It's all right.'

Of course nobody moved. Suddenly the little girl ran down the dunes towards the hut. 'I'm coming,' she said. For a moment there was panic! Some people tried to run after the little girl to get her back, while some of the younger ones were trying to join her. Pandemonium broke loose, but not for long. Four or five of the villagers went into the hut and saw it was all right. Candles had been lit and there was tea brewing on the stove. The others joined them and everyone was made most welcome. There was laughter and much warmth and kindness.

After a while one of the younger men plucked up his courage and asked, 'Please, tell us what you were doing there on the beach? What is the sound that we all heard that was like the wind in the pine trees? There are no trees here. What was the cracking like thunder and what are these designs on the sand that we have heard about?'

Few had ever heard the old man speak before. He smiled, and his voice was as gentle as mountain rain. It almost seemed to come from beyond time. 'So you want to know what I have been doing after all these years! Of course you are right to question, but remember, nothing happens unless the time is right. I have waited here for many years until someone would come to see me and ask that question. And when the time was right, this young man came. I have been polishing my heart, making it shine brightly like a mirror, so that when one day someone came, they could look into that mirror and thus see themselves. The sound of the wind in the trees is the sound of the polish gliding over the surface and the sound of the thunder is the breaking open of my own heart so that this young man can see what lies inside.'

'But what *is* this sound we hear?' one of the people asked. 'Ah,' the old man replied, 'that is the sound of *hū*. It is the most sacred sound in the universe. You can hear it everywhere for it brings with it the Message of God.'

Then a silence filled the hut. The villagers were quiet. They were ashamed that they had thought the old man was mad, for now, somewhere deep inside each of their hearts, a flame had been lit. There was nothing strange anymore. The only sounds they could hear were the gentle breakers on the sand and the crackling of the wood fire. A great peace had settled in the hut. The stars shone brighter than they had ever done before.

By the time the first light of dawn was spreading across the horizon, touching the breakers on the sand, the old man and the young man had gone. The villagers never saw them again. The hut remained but the symbols were washed away in the ebb and flow of the tides.

From that moment on strange things started to happen. One of the men in the village went to live in the hut and soon he was able to teach the rest how to polish their own mirrors and how to hear the *Hū* in their own hearts. He couldn't quite say how he knew but one day he started talking and what he said was right. Some people noticed that his voice sounded strangely like the old man's. A new brotherhood grew up in the village. Even the old ladies stopped gossiping in the store on Saturday mornings and the children looked bright and radiant as moonbeams.

No one ever discovered what happened to the old man. Years later, when one of the villagers was travelling abroad on his holidays, for a moment he thought he saw the young man sitting in a café. Yet, he couldn't be sure, for when he looked very hard, a shiny mirror appeared and he saw himself in the evening sun.

4

BREATH AND WORKING WITH THEMES

'Without a question we are only half alive. Who
am I? What is the purpose of life on earth?'

This is a book composed not only of stories, but of ideas. There is a whole world of ideas, much of which has been kept guarded and secret in the past. There was a valid reason for this in that ideas contain great power in themselves. Of course it is what we do with them that matters. Like everything else, they can be misused. In earlier times these ideas were given only to a select few, but times have changed dramatically and now more and more information is being given to help us on the way.

Twenty years ago I started to teach a particular rhythm of breathing. The method actually came from a very ancient tradition but after experimenting with it for a long time myself, I became convinced that it was perfectly safe to give to other people. When I first published it in my books, however, I found myself in much trouble. I received endless letters and telephone calls demanding where I had found this knowledge and what right I had to share this with all and sundry. Some people were even angry. It was as though I was releasing esoteric secrets which they felt that they, or the group they worked with, almost owned as a personal treasure. Eventually it all calmed down and indeed the knowledge has proven to be beneficial. The rhythm of the breathing practice, that is the 7–1–7–1–7 breathing (see Addendum), is now being used in hospitals and clinics all over the world.

Everything that I teach is thoroughly applicable in our daily lives. The practices of visualisation and conscious breathing can help us to function to our full capacity as human beings, for the benefit of the whole. But we must not be too serious. Knowledge without humour would surely make the world an almost impossible place in which to live!

One day, at a seminar in California, I had been teaching the breathing practice and the art of visualisation all morning. For the lunch-break I had given a theme for all the participants to work with. Working with themes is another method that is used in this path of transformation. A similar method is used in Zen Buddhism when the Master gives what is called a *koan*, which is a challenging question for the pupil to contemplate – for example: 'What is the sound of one hand clapping?' It is the same in working with themes. A theme is given to be worked with for a specific length of time, or, for some themes, there is a never-ending question. Such a theme could be 'What is the purpose of life on earth?'

The theme on that day was just one word which everyone was asked to hold in their hearts. It was the one word *'noticing'*. I had gone to great lengths to point out that most of our lives we do not notice things very deeply. We get so used to daily life that we presume too much. Noticing something in all of its many facets is a beautiful art form. If we walk along the beach and notice only the sand we will miss the abalone shells!

Noticing requires that we use our eyes to look through rather than just from. This brings an entirely new dimension to life. It is said in the Sufi Tradition, 'I am the eyes through which God sees. I am the ears through which God hears.' I wonder who is seeing and hearing what! Life does take on a very different meaning when we are awake enough to notice things, not on their face value, but *le dedans des choses*, the within-ness of things.

Visualisation without breath is like a pen without ink and noticing without being awake to the breath is only half the true picture. It is also important that we do not try too hard. There is right effort and there is wrong effort. Right effort is not made merely for ourselves but for the good of the whole. Wrong effort can bring about what is sometimes called a reverse spiral. This is surely not difficult to understand but we do have to question ourselves continuously about such matters lest we bring about unnecessary chaos in our own lives and into the world.

That is why I spent all morning explaining how everyone could benefit by working with the theme of *noticing* and reminded them that they needed to be awake to the breath and even visualise themselves noticing that they were noticing! Just before the lunch-break I asked that when we reassembled people would tell me if they had noticed anything unusual or what might appear to be unusual. Since we also work very much with the nature of time, I insisted that everyone return slightly early so that we could start the next class precisely at the agreed time.

It so happened that all of the seventy people did arrive well in time for the next class and I could not help noticing that one young lady had her arm bandaged and in a sling. Perhaps she had arrived that morning in the same condition and I had not noticed. It did seem a trifle strange. Anyway, we started off with the usual breathing practice, bringing everyone into the present moment, and then I asked if anyone had anything to report. The lady with the sling was the first to stand up. She was smiling a little sheepishly but there was a twinkle in her eye.

She told us her story. She had gone with four friends to a restaurant for lunch, desperately trying to notice everything. As she admitted, they had all forgotten about breathing consciously in the rhythm that they had been taught during the morning and they were trying so hard to notice that they had virtually gone to sleep. I can just imagine them all staring around from the table where they were sitting, trying to make mental notes of what they were seeing. And that is not noticing. That is making a series of static images for their mental notebooks. In fact, they tried so hard that they must have built up a strong electromagnetic field around where they were sitting which then produced disastrous results.

A well-meaning waiter, carrying a tray of glasses in one hand above his shoulder, came towards their table, ran into this vortex of backwards energy and to his surprise, lost his presence of mind and dropped the whole tray. Broken glasses were scattered everywhere and, of course, the whole restaurant turned round and noticed what was going on! Unfortunately one of the glasses fell in such a way that a piece of glass cut one of her wrists right into the artery. So now there was blood and broken glass. More chaos! Everyone rushed around, a tourniquet was applied and they all left for the hospital in a great hurry. They had not even had time to order their meal.

Arriving at the hospital, the lady with the tourniquet was quickly shown into the emergency room. A nurse came up to her. 'Sit down quietly,' she said. 'Try to keep your back as straight as possible. Now I want you to breathe gently to this rhythm. Breathe in to the count of seven, pause, and then breathe out to the count of seven . . .' It turned out that the nurse had been a former pupil of mine! Of course she also knew the rules about time and the doctor was summoned so that the injured lady could get back to the seminar in time for the next class! Stitches were quickly applied, we were told as the story unfolded, the lady still smiling despite the troubles, and she arrived back to start the class with us all, a little sore perhaps, but having learned a great lesson about noticing, or we might say, how *not* to notice.

The whole idea of working with themes is an ancient one. This relative world of form is given to us as a frame to see through into the real world. When we are given a theme, we awaken questions which have remained dormant for so long. We need the experience of life to realise that this world is, indeed, merely a world of appearances. Thus we start to question the nature of the real world, this world beyond time and space as we know it. Like the Breath of Everlasting Life, Truth cannot be limited by the prison that is this transient life of ours. Yet it is not far away. It is merely the illusion of separation from our Creator that, for most of our lives, makes it seem impossible to come to realise.

We will always be confronted with only half of the answer if we cannot remember the sacredness of our breath. Themes can produce many challenging questions for us, yet theoretical answers alone will never satisfy us. We need to live in the eternal question concerning the nature of who and what we are.

5

TIME COUNTS

*'The world of reality is not the world of
appearances. Just remember that what you see
is not what it really is. The whole key to
identification is that if you have a friend who
can wake you up, say thank you.'*

As I have already said, all that I teach can be put to
use in everyday life. Working with themes, the breath,
visualisation etc., does not make life necessarily easier
but these methods bring a deeper meaning to life. So
often we just presume life. We presume that we are
going to wake up in the morning, go to work as usual,
and come back again in the evening to our families. In
that human presumption we are not open to the miracles
that are around us all the time. Perhaps one day we will
not wake up one morning and most of our lives will have
been wasted. The inner secrets will have passed us by,
the outer appearances of life having been our only reality.
The beauty of Unity will have evaded us, although it was
offered all the time. What we see of time, this life that
starts from conception, goes through birth to death, is
only one aspect of what, in Truth, is Everlasting Life.
'Time is the eternal attribute of God,' it is said.

There are other ways to look at time. There are the
cycles of time in the natural world bringing in the seasons,
spring followed by summer, autumn and winter. There is
the vastness of time when we can only measure distance
in light-years. It has always been said, until very recently,
that nothing can go faster than the speed of light, i.e.
186,000 miles per second. Now some scientists have
measured a pulsar speeding away out of the universe at

a speed faster than light. It is a vast world, this world of ours, and our life is a beautiful journey of discovery.

As well as the time that apparently moves from the past through the present into the unknown future, there is also the time that is moving from the completion of the experiment of life on earth back through the present moment to redeem what is still left in the wilderness of the past. And there is still another type of space–time relationship which is invisible to our normal senses, but which is available to us to be understood if we could only see. In order to see with other and deeper senses than the ones we are familiar with, of taste, touch, smell, hearing and sight, we surely do need to be on top of the breath, consciously seeking the purpose of life on earth.

I describe this invisible kingdom as being of a different geometry to ours. In this kingdom are all the creatures of the elements, invisible to the naked eye but still there. We read about them in all the classical legends and fairy stories. We have all heard about 'the little people', the guardians who watch over the plants and animals, and the custodians of the mountains. We have heard how magicians used to put their treasure in a cave and then place a sentinel over it to protect it for ever. This could appear in the form of a snake, or, if the cave was under the ocean, perhaps an enormous octopus. Most people see these legends as just entertainment for children to keep magic in the air, but maybe that is not entirely true.

I have a story to illustrate this. It is a magical story and one that I could never forget. Of course you can believe it or not. It is up to you.

Many years ago I was running a community centre in the English countryside. That it all worked as it did was a miracle in itself and I cannot but imagine that we had invisible helpers in every step that we took. You see, whenever we are totally committed, the inhabitants of these kingdoms come running to help us: strange things occur, and there is no logical explanation for them; people turn up to help just when they are needed, as though guided by invisible forces. As we remember to be always of service to our children and our children's children, we bring in this other aspect of time, sharing the same adventure.

It was hard work building the Centre as well as giving lectures both in England and in the States, and it was a rare occasion when there was a little free time. On the day of this story I was in London. There were just two hours in between one appointment and another and so I decided to take a walk along the streets of London and to visit a particular bookshop that was a favourite of mine. It was one of those beautiful spring days when everything seems much lighter and brighter than normal. The air was effervescent. It seemed to bubble like the finest champagne.

As I walked along I was musing on *Khidr*, known as the guide of the Sufis. This invisible guide is mentioned in all traditions. In the Celtic history he is called 'the Green Man' since he often appears dressed in green. There are even pubs named after him! There is always the inner guide but this Khidr very often manifests himself in physical form to guide us along in most strange and marvellous ways. In the Centre we had been reading stories on the subject but I had personally never expected to meet this strange man. Remember, Khidr comes to guide us and to help us.

At that period of the building of the Centre we were very short of money and naturally I was worried about this. But it was such a beautiful day I had forgotten my worries, or had I? I was in the heart of London, Piccadilly Circus, and the bookshop wasn't far away. There was a small crowd gathered on the street corner. People were peering over each other's shoulders and I joined the throng to see what was going on. In fact it was a group of men gambling on the turn of three cards. It is a famous and extremely crooked game, illegal in England. I saw that there were look-out men placed to watch for the police. Hundreds of pounds were changing hands. It was fascinating. The man behind the box which served as a table would take the three cards and show them face-up. One of them was always the jack. And then he would deftly turned them round and place the cards face-down on the box in front of him. You had to guess which card was the jack. Having seen them face-up, it seemed obvious which one the card would be. If someone wanted to bet, they would put their money in cash on top of the card that they thought was the jack. In ninety cases out of one hundred they were wrong.

I was fascinated! How was this done? As I was asking myself this question, I became aware of a tall man standing on my left. There was something strange about him. He emanated a certain presence which was totally magnetic. When he turned round to me, he spoke in a Scottish accent. Was it by chance that I was going to Scotland the next week to visit another centre in Edinburgh?

'Do ye know how they do it?' he said, in his thick brogue. 'Well, I'll tell you. Just you watch me.' With that, as the cards were turned down, he took £30 from his pocket and put the money on the card. He won! I had watched the cards as well and I could have sworn that the jack was not the card he had put his money on. It was a strange day.

'You see,' he went on, looking at me. 'It's all done so fast that you can't see what he does. As he puts the card down, the jack is where you thought it was, but it takes a little time for you to get your money out of your pocket and to lean over to put it on the cards. Just then, if you watch carefully, someone is distracting you, and the man moves the cards again.'

It was time for the next game. I stared, making every effort I could to keep awake to each split second. Down came the cards and to my total surprise, the Scotsman lent forward, stuck his finger on a card, handed me £30 with the other hand and said, 'Put it on that one!' I hadn't time to think. I did what I was told and won £30. Of course I tried to give it back to him. He smiled at me. 'No, it's yours my friend. You won it.'

'But it was your money,' I said. 'Really, thank you but I don't need it.' I thanked him again, handing back the money, and walked on towards the bookshop.

There was the same atmosphere of unworldliness as I reached the shop. Precisely at the moment I entered the door, an old friend from New York was just walking out and we bumped into each other. 'So there you are,' we both said. He was on his way from the airport to the Centre! 'Come along then,' I said. 'Let's go and have a beer somewhere.' We walked back towards Piccadilly and I told him the strange goings-on with the Scotsman. 'I promise you it's true,' I said. 'Look, I'll show you where he is.'

We came around the corner. It could not have been five minutes since I was there. The man was gone; the crowd was gone; the box being used as a table was gone. Everything had disappeared. 'Oh, I suppose the police came,' I said. But I had a very strange prickly feeling going up and down my back. Had the morning been real at all?

We walked on, talking about mutual interests. I was not very awake, in all the excitement of seeing my friend, and suddenly a young man, his head down, bumped straight into me. I think I was upset for a brief moment, but then realised that it was another friend, who was actually staying at the Centre. He was in London looking for a special ring for his fiancée. He was shortly to be married and had been given the task of finding this ring by a Zoroastrian priest in order to test his intuitive faculties.

We all walked on. Time was taking on a different meaning for I only had two hours all told, and, looking at my watch, hardly any time had passed by. We went up a passageway where cars were not allowed and there, on the side of the road, was a beggar. I remember he hadn't shaved for a couple of days and had only one leg. I always try and remember charity and so it was really without thinking I put my hand in my pocket and gave him whatever I had. The three of us were probably still talking. I did not even look at the beggar's face.

As we passed on, he called out to me. 'Excuse me, sir,' he said. 'That is very kind of you, but could you do me a favour?'

'Well, of course,' I said, without even asking him what it was. I suppose it could have been anything!

'Could you please get me some fish and chips?' Not being in the habit of going to fish and chip shops, I wasn't sure where to go. He explained that we were to walk up one street, cross over, turn left and then we would find it.

Off we went as if all this was perfectly normal for a spring day in London. We found the fish shop. In fact, we smelled it a long way away. I asked for the best fish and chips the man could give me. My friends and I were still talking as I was handed a beautifully wrapped parcel. I had always thought the fish and chips in England were wrapped in newspaper. In fact they normally are to this day. I asked him how much. 'Forty-nine p,' he said. I was dumbfounded. Why that figure? It is, and was, a number concerning the matrix, part of the invisible counterpart of man, that I had been studying for months.

Just at that moment the warm parcel in my hand turned into a dove. No, you do not have to believe it, but for me it was a dove. I could not speak and my friends didn't seem to notice anything. I looked again and it was the parcel of fish and chips. I changed gear, as it were, and went back into that other world, and there was the dove again. I could feel its warm breast in the palm of my hand.

Telling my friends to remain where they were, I hastened back to where the beggar had been sitting on the side of the road. I handed him the parcel, totally unable to do anything but feel a sense of awe and wonder. A door had been opened for me. 'Thank you,' said the beggar, handing me forty-nine pence.

This time I looked at him. He was the same man as the Scotsman. True, there were two different bodies, but it was the same being without any doubt. How could he have known that the fish and chips would have cost forty-nine pence? There were many different prices. Why had this all happened? The man smiled at me, one of those great big warm smiles that seems to contain a very deep understanding. I smiled back in acknowledgement and went back to join my friends.

Over lunch I telephoned Hamid, the man I had accepted as being my Teacher and Spiritual Guide at that time. I was still totally overwhelmed with the events that had taken place that morning and I explained, as briefly as I could, what had transpired. I must have sounded very nervous and agitated! 'You'd better come on round immediately,' he said. 'I will cancel my appointments. This has been an important time for you.'

It was over an hour later when I told him word for word what had happened. Hamid listened carefully, occasionally stopping me to check on some detail or another. He was warm and friendly, and I remember he had a slight twinkle in his eyes as he listened. Eventually he got up from his chair and put his hand on my shoulder.

'Ah, Reshad,' he said, 'indeed that was a very good sign, for that Being you met, disguised in two different bodies, was Khidr, the Guide. Why do you think he appeared as he did? Why was there such a lot of mention of money in both stories? How could the man have known the exact cost of the fish and chips when there are many varieties you could have chosen, all costing different amounts? Remember, I told you not to worry weeks ago and that what you needed would be provided for at the right time. But you continued to worry and so Khidr came to show you that worrying is a pointless waste of time.'

'But what about the dove?' I asked him. 'It was a dove. I *know* it was!'

'You must ask yourself what a dove represents to you,' Hamid said, 'and then you will understand. You see, we are all given what we need in so many different ways. We must be awake and look to the signs. They are great gifts. I have always told you that this is a world of appearances. Most probably the dove represented a symbol of peace, and it was peace in understanding that you were looking for, just as you wanted peace from all the worries concerning the money.'

That was the end of our conversation. Three weeks later the money for the Centre was donated by some people I scarcely knew.

6

PASSING TRAINS

'Normally we are not awake to time coming in.
We are only aware of time moving on.'

When we are completely committed to life itself, many things can happen to us, some of which seem almost inexplicable. But we need to remember always that each individual is unique and therefore no two experiences can ever be exactly the same. The story that I have just told to illustrate something about the other worlds was given to me as an experience that was necessary at that moment of time on my own spiritual journey. I did not ask for it. It came as an act of Grace. Since everyone is uniquely different, there are some people truly awake already who do not have such mysterious adventures. They are not necessary for everyone and that is why it is always stressed that we must not copy another. 'Repeat not spiritually what others have done before you,' Sri Aurobindo, a great Indian mystic, once said.

We must not crave experience. We might believe in someone else's life so deeply that we would even have a pale copy of that person's life manifested in our own. And yet it would not be wholly real. It would not be ours. It would be a watered-down version of something in another time and space. Many people have not believed the story of Khidr when I have told it. It was not in their reality to believe it. We have to be as adaptable as water to flow with the moment and trust such things. I would add that the lady in the first story bore no grudge or resentment from the cut wrist. Far from it! She was already a wise woman and became even wiser from the event. We get everything we need to fulfil our lives, but not necessarily everything we want.

Now we come to another aspect of time and that is the time we actually can create ourselves through the art of visualisation. Again it is very important to understand in order to become complete in ourselves. It is said that God is pulling on the rope to bring us home but that we have to climb it by making all right efforts in a life of service.

The easiest way to see how we can create another sort of time is by looking at the results of our own negative emotions and thinking. We all know that negativity comes back to us eventually, but we do not exactly know *when*. Sometimes the results are quickly seen. At other times, perhaps even years later, we suddenly wake up to a mistake we have made in the past which has gone out into the future and is now coming back on us. It has to come back to us because those negative thought-forms actually want to be redeemed. They don't like it 'out there' and it is only through the present moment that that which we have projected into the future can be redeemed. It is the same with past time. The two meet in the present moment.

We can be quite sure that all our negativity will come back to roost one day and it is better to work on ourselves continuously, staying in the present moment and breathing consciously, than to wait for the inevitable chaos that will ensue if we do not. We cannot expect others to do it for us. It is in our own uniqueness, given our own life and set of experiences, that we are asked to participate in the Great Plan, which has been called, 'the experiment of life on earth'. With true commitment comes freedom and finally knowledge, and it is knowledge that anchors love. Love without knowledge is only half of the picture and God wants us to understand His Unity and His Uniqueness.

Let us look at the truly creative aspect of the time that we can create through visualisation. A great deal of this has to be taken on trust in the first stages. However, there is a simple practice that everyone can do each day which most surely can help to bring about a better life.

We take one day at a time. We realise that this may
be the only day we have. We want to fill it up with all
the good things as well as working on all those aspects
of ourselves which certainly need working on! We agree
that we do not want to remain stuck in the limitations of
our own horizons. We want to be free!

I often teach this method in a seminar. A group of
people come together and once the rhythm of the breath
is established, I ask everyone to visualise the end of the
time that we have agreed to be together during that day,
but *at the same time* remembering when the day started and
also being awake to the present moment in the relative
world. One of the easiest ways to visualise these times is
by internally seeing a big clock on the wall with the hands
pointing to the respective times. It is not so difficult to do
as long as we are breathing alive! Let's say that the day
together was due to finish at 5.00 p.m., that the seminar
started at 10.00 a.m., and by the time everyone got into
the rhythm of the breath it was 11.00 a.m. We would have
these three times to remember at the same moment. Each
person would be asked to enquire within whether he or
she was committed to that day. Then we would all take
one deep breath, holding it in the visualisation, and gently
let it go. The play of the day had begun.

In the deepest sense of visualisation and commitment,
creating this aspect of time ourselves, whatever happens,
can be seen to be part of the play of life. Since nothing
happens by chance, we can begin to see the inner
meaning of the signs that we are given. Fish and chips
was not necessarily fish and chips! However, we find that
our false greed and ambition are subtly taken away and we
are brought into a deep sense of gratefulness by the end
of the day. There is a sound of gratefulness. Of course it
does not mean to say that the day is going to be all easy,
all roses. There are no roses without pruning! But when
we do all part after those hours together, having worked
hard to stay on the breath and in the present moment,
we know that something real has been accomplished.
There is something permanent growing in our inner
work. Ultimately we can see that if we could visualise

our own death, knowing that this is the only life that we have, then life itself would take on an entirely different meaning and purpose to the average sleepwalker, who is just carried around by the ebb and tide of fate. We need not be subjected to fate alone if we can remember these different aspects of time, all carried in the Breath of Life.

When we take one day at a time, bringing in all these aspects of time, it is as though there are two trains moving towards each other. One is the train coming from the past, already set in motion from the moment of our birth, the driver steaming ahead, stoking the engine with the fuel of unredeemed thought-forms. Then, waiting out there at the end of the day is another train. The engine is ready, powered by a very fine fuel indeed, and the driver sits, waiting patiently until he gets the signal to set the train in motion. This only happens when we have agreed to our commitment. The moment he gets the message, he puts the train in gear. His train comes from completion through a world of possibility. The compartments are filled with helpers, waiting for the first train to get closer. They finally pass on the wind of the present moment. Mevlana Jelaluddin Rumi, a great Persian poet and mystic, said, 'I know that the two worlds are One.' We know this when the two trains pass. We could say that the driver of the train coming in, and the one going out, would both be able to wave to the station-master at the same time!

7

BREATHE IN – BREATHE OUT

'If the breath is limited, life is limited.'

Patience is surely one of the names of God! For me, it has been one of the most difficult lessons to learn. All of us in the West suffer from the dreaded disease of expectation, which stems from an educational background geared to give us this disease. We have examinations to pass, grades to be numbered and counted, and a sense that there is a reward just around the corner for all of our hard work. Everyone knows perfectly well that money does not necessarily bring happiness, inner peace and contentment and yet our whole system is based on the acquisition of it. Today cultures can topple on the drop of the stock market. What a ridiculous situation! How then can we readjust our thinking in order to understand the path of transformation and our direct responsibility for it? It is a good question.

We breathe in only to breathe out. It is relatively easy to remember how to breathe in. We all love to breathe in the aroma of sweet perfumes or the smell of the ocean. We can breathe in the passion of the moment. We can visualise a colour and irradiate ourselves with it. We can breathe in strength and courage. We can sense the gentleness of a flower on the in-breath.

And there is also another aspect of the in-breath. If we are not awake, we may breathe in the results of our own negative emotions or thoughts and even share in those of others. We breathe in thoughts held in the moisture of the breath.

Let me explain it this way. We have seen that when we enter a room, we are all breathing the same air. If you could measure the air in the room before and after a business meeting, for example, it would be different indeed. Certainly the atmosphere would have changed and the atmosphere comes from the moisture contained in the breath. The atmosphere in a church, a mosque or a temple normally has beautiful vibrations. People go to these places to pray, to ask, in humility, for what is needed. They praise God on the out-breath with their singing and chanting. They are not frightened to breathe out, filling their world with love and light. In an atmosphere that is filled with greed, there is endless talking and negotiating, but very little giving. Thus there is imbalance. It is so important to remember the out-breath. We are given so much in life, and it is on the breath that we can give away to our friends and to the very planet itself.

If you open your arms, first to the side, and then bring them up above your head, the hands touching, and finally bring them forward in an arc, the fingers touching and the arms extended in front of the centre of the chest, you have defined your own universe. In other words, your universe is within the extent of your armspan. Imagine your hands as being the extension of your heart centre so that you could stretch out and breathe through your hands as well as your nostrils! You could touch a beautiful leaf or a flower and in recognition of its beauty, breathe in. Then you could breathe out the essence of the beauty that you have breathed in, thus filling up your universe with love and light. You truly have something to give.

The trouble is that we find, if we are truly honest, that the vibrations on the out-breath do not travel very far, rarely as far as the extent of our own arm-span. It is as though we have been so stifled and repressed in our lives that the pain is somehow trapped. Yet, if we breathe in beauty, pain can be transformed and then the out-breath is pure, moving out into a waiting world.

What happens between the in-breath and the out-breath? The reality of the moment stands right in the middle of those two breaths and it is only when they are truly balanced that we can know what lies hidden there. If the two breaths are not balanced, that which wants so desperately to be released remains imprisoned within our hearts. That is why the teaching of conscious breathing is so important. We can fill up our heads with conceptual thinking but the prison doors remain locked.

The first time I came upon this idea I was living in a Zen Buddhist monastery in Japan. I was young and perhaps that was why the importance of the balance of the two breaths did not mean enough to me so that I would really work to perfect the breath. Many years later I went on a retreat to another monastery, this time run by Tibetan Buddhists. I went with every expectation in the world, deciding I was definitely going to find an answer to my questions. We were told, when we arrived, that if we wanted an interview with the Lama, we must sign our name on a waiting list. We would then have twenty minutes of his valuable time. I signed up immediately, and a few days later I was told when I could see him.

I remember going into the Lama's room in a state that could be described as a mixture of expectation and sheer terror. He was sitting on a cushion and indicated that I was to sit opposite him. He spoke very little English, which did not make life any easier. I tried to explain my problems. He just looked and smiled, nodding frequently. I don't think he really understood a word, but it didn't seem to matter. Towards the end of the allotted twenty minutes he said, 'Very good. You breathe in only to breathe out. You start today, six hours please . . .' The interview was over.

I went back to my little room, trying to get used to the idea. I had come a long way and all I was told was that it was necessary to sit down and breathe for six solid hours every day. No further explanation was offered. I didn't even know what a lotus sitting position was, and of course there were no chairs in the meditation hall.

There were about twenty-five people staying in the Centre and, at that time, several visiting Lamas, who started chanting soon after 4.00 a.m., when we were all meant to get up and begin our meditations. I hadn't the slightest idea what they were chanting. There were a lot of bells and gongs which were struck at appropriate moments. It was all very mysterious but after a few days I settled into the rhythm and things quietened down considerably.

Those six hours of breathing were still worrying me! Luckily I had been provided with a hard, round cushion to sit on and I knew that I was meant to keep my back as straight as possible. I plucked up courage and went down to the meditation hall. It was dark, lit only by candles. The air was thick with the smell of incense. In the gloom I could see about ten other people sitting and, presumably, breathing. It was very difficult not to feel self-conscious in such a situation.

I felt hopelessly naïve, but closing my eyes, I began. Breathe in. Breathe out! I cannot remember just how long I sat there that first day. I reckoned that it was all right to divide the six hours into sections. Anyway, my legs went to sleep, my back hurt and nothing happened at all. I do not know what I expected but whatever it was surely did not materialise. There were no bright lights, no flashes of understanding. There was, however, a lot of rumbling in the stomach area I remember, because the food was not to my taste at all.

I got through the first day and steeled myself to start all over again the next. Luckily there was one man I could talk to and we went for a walk that evening. He was equally English but had been working at this practice for some years. He was very courteous and patient with me and told me to persevere.

To cut a long story short, I persevered breathing in and breathing out for six hours a day for a whole week and then I asked to see the Lama again. This time there was a translator, which helped matters considerably. I tried to explain, as politely as possible, that I had breathed, that I found it impossibly difficult to remain awake, that thoughts kept crowding in from all sides and that so far nothing had happened! 'Ah-ha,' said the Lama. 'Very good. Now eight hours a day please.' The translator smiled, the Lama smiled and I tried to smile. Now it was to be eight hours of sitting in that same meditation hall, with a lot of silent people all around me and that dreaded incense. Again I went back to my room to try to recover.

I will say that the next week was very different. Expectation had gone out of the window. In its place came utter and complete boredom! It is true that the breathing was becoming easier and the balance was better, but fitting eight hours into the day was a hard task indeed. The following week the Lama increased the time once more and that was when something started changing. I found myself as though hallucinating. It seemed that every fear and guilt I had ever had started to emerge. The fears manifested in physical pictures. I could swear there were snakes and tigers in the room. I was in a jungle. Finally I was so terrified I asked to see the Lama urgently. This time he looked even happier, smiling and nodding vehemently, when I explained the story to him. He then laughed out loud saying, 'Very good, very good! Continue!'

I did continue. Little by little the fears went and there was a dancing sensation in the breath. All the thought pictures disappeared as they were redeemed through the present moment, and I was beginning to get a taste of what it could mean to be on top of the breath. Time took on a totally different meaning. There were even moments when a flash of real understanding would come. When I saw the Lama in the passageway, he would bow and smile. I did not go to see him again. I knew for certain he had been right all along.

8

A Thought in the Mind of God

'There is no freedom in thinking.'

Perhaps the most important lesson from my experiences with the Tibetan Lama was a furthering of the under-standing of transformation and of what it is that needs to be transformed. We return, once more, to the subject of the element of water and its subtle connection to thought-form.

Everyone knows perfectly well that there are times when we cannot see or hear clearly. It is like a hang-over of the thoughts of the day before, or maybe over many years. Nearly all thinking is based upon comparison, and in comparison there can be no understanding of Unity.

There is a saying that is often used as a challenge to aspiring pupils of the esoteric path: 'Ever since the time of the Virgin Mary, there is no more need to think.' I have used this statement many times in working with themes to illustrate how it is up to the individual, by endless yearning in the question, to discover the hidden meaning in the words. Every parable, every Sufi story has at least seven levels of meaning, each one growing deeper into understanding as we go deeper and deeper into the breath. However, it is important not to *think* about the answer.

Some years ago, on my yearly German tour, one of the great misquotes of all time occurred. I have to rely on translators and it is naturally very difficult to translate such a sentence as the one above. It is difficult enough to understand even the outer meaning in English.

I was on the stage with my translator, a dear German friend, and there were several hundred people in the hall. Up to that point the evening had gone very well. I recollect I was talking about the Line of the Prophets in the Sufi Tradition and how it is considered that there

are twenty-seven major prophets from the beginning of
time, starting with Adam, and going right through to the
completion of the line of prophets as seen in the Prophet
Muhammad (peace and blessing be upon him and his
family). I was saying that, in that tradition, both Jesus
and Mary are considered to be in the line of the prophets.
It was at that time that I made the quote: 'Ever since the
time of the Virgin Mary, there is no more need to think.'
I turned to the translator whilst he mulled over the
sentence, trying to find a suitable way to interpret such
a statement. There was a pause, and a very definite hush
fell on the hall. Most German people have at least a little
understanding of English. I fear my friend was thinking
too much for, after the pause, when you could hear a
pin drop, he announced, 'Reshad says that ever since the
time of the Virgin Mary there is no more need for virgins!'

Laughter is a great healer, perhaps one of the best
ways, for it is another word for breath. Most surely it helps
the out-breath. All those hundreds of people just couldn't
contain themselves. They laughed and laughed and the
day was saved. There is always a danger that people can
get too serious on the spiritual path.

What is thought? What is its purpose and what is a
'thought-form'? These are eternal questions, the subjects
of endless discussions and arguments. For me the spiritual quest has never excluded this subject. So many
people seem to make their own separate journey towards
Truth, excluding all the rest of life, whereas, in reality we
cannot separate anything from the whole if we wish to
understand Unity, come into Unity and share in the great
adventure that we call life.

Thought is a necessary part of the process and yet
thinking is about as dangerous an occupation as could
be imagined. Look at the trouble it has got us into. Look
at our own lives and how we have been led astray
by false hopes and dreams, all based on the nature of
thought.

Yet thought, in essence, is pure energy. Consider
what it would feel like when you were merely a thought in
the Mind of God. It would be pure thought, pure energy,

available and useful for the world, not fragmented into a myriad of shattered dreams. Jesus said, in the Apocryphal Acts of John, 'I am thought, being wholly thought.' Surely he was saying that he was, and is, a thought in the Mind of God. He expressed the Divine; he continuously remembered the Unity and the interconnectedness of all life.

Imagine thought like a spoonful of mercury, of quick-silver, as it is called. First there was a spoon, held in the hand of God. And then, whether by accident or not, the spoon was tipped over and the mercury fell out onto the ground, splitting into endless pieces and forming numerous patterns on the ground. Perhaps the tipping of the spoon was necessary, otherwise there would be no play, no stage of life and no players!

The journey is toward our homeland and so it takes one little piece of mercury to start to gather up all the other pieces scattered across the surface of the globe. Slowly, step by step, effort after effort, we gather up the thought-forms, longing to be brought together into one cohesive whole, and then Unity is understood. It is gained by right effort, work in the right direction. It does not happen merely by chance.

Now the key to the gathering up of these fractured pieces of energy, as elusive as mercury itself, is to do with the very nature of breath itself. Were we ever told as children that the word 'breath' comes from the same root in Greek as the word 'spirit'? Try transposing the two words. Whenever you hear the word spirit, remember the breath and whenever you are conscious of the breath, remember the spirit. That alone can make a profound difference in our lives. Breath *is* life.

At times I have seen myself rather like a stagnant pond, the mind going round and round upon itself, each thought trying to find just one partner. Then there have been times when there was a flowing of the water of life, the spirit 'moving on the face of the waters', and harmony would prevail. Others would feel this harmony and react to it and people would even find themselves in the flow once again. Yet, when I forgot the breath, the spirit, back again came the stagnant pond. The mind would follow and then the emotions and finally the body itself and there would be sickness. This is the same for us all.

The breath moves; the spirit moves. The water starts to flow back towards the ocean once again. There is freedom. There is joy. There is a sense of the final completion that is the heritage of the soul. No more are we bound by the shackles of illusion when no one thought has a partner, when there is the desperate loneliness that we have all experienced.

Breath is life. We breathe in only to breathe out. We are given this great gift that we can understand thought and the process of thought, the transposition of thought from one world to another, from the world of pure thought to the world of fixed archetypes, to the world of ideas, through the world of possibilities and right down into the relative world, continuously waiting to be born in each conscious moment of breath taken by a human being.

And yet evolution is not just a simple matter of the continuation of life on earth. There is organic evolution and there is conscious evolution, or at least the possibility of conscious evolution. Organic evolution is in the natural order of things but it is up to man and woman to take the great step into conscious evolution. By this I mean that we have to be conscious, loving, kind and aware participants in the interconnectedness of all life, not just swept along by the tides of fate. Destiny can be in the hands of a lover. Fate is in the hands of the forgetful.

Look at the state the world is in now. Everywhere we see pollution, sickness, greed and illusion. It has not always been this way. However, history does go in cycles, and now, in our time, we surely have enough warnings to move us to want to work for our children and our children's children so that they can grow up in a world of reawakened possibility. It is up to us. No one can do it for us. We need to learn how to breathe, why to breathe, what breath is and why it is given to us that there is life on earth. We can talk and talk, and think and think, but what is the point if we cannot realise that once we *were* a thought in the Mind of God, and it is to the One that we return. 'The One creates the two, the two the three, and the three the ten thousand things.' So it says in the Tao, the Tao that *is* life!

9

THE TRIAD OF FREEDOM

*'Without true commitment there is merely a
repetition of something that needs to be
redeemed rather than repeated.'*

In many of my lectures and workshops I talk about something I term 'the Triad of Freedom'. Just as the one creates
the two, the two the three and the three the ten thousand
things, so there is a triad of freedom which helps us to
make good use of unredeemed thought-form. I call this
the triad of 'Commitment, Willingness and Agreement',
and it is the understanding of the inner meaning of the
words that can bring about real change, rather than just
the apparency of change.

We have seen that, due to the fact that we are 80
per cent water, we collect a mass of mostly useless
thought-forms, and then it is a wonder that we can
think at all, let alone think creatively for the good of the
whole and for our children and our children's children.
After all, if we are merely repeating habit patterns, due to
our identification with thoughts of the past, we are really
doing very little towards the whole process of conscious
evolution. Conscious breathing helps to bring about the
flow necessary for real change to come about. We also
need to have understanding as to how breath can literally
change our lives. This is where the triad of freedom
becomes so important.

Pure thought is pure energy. If it is a projection of
second-hand thought, then it is not pure energy. If we
look honestly and deeply into our own lives we will see
how often we start a particular project, or make plans for
a journey, without being totally committed to the idea. Of
course there are many levels of commitment, just as there

are many worlds. We can be committed to an ideal, and then an idea, and so on down the scale into materialisation of the ideal. However, there is hazard and danger at every step and so it is vitally important that the degree of our commitment is of the highest order. Otherwise, we can be led astray so easily from our original intention.

There is always a portion of ourselves which wants to hold back, to hang onto anything that offers us some sort of security or support. It is like the story of the pupil who asks his Teacher to take him to the Truth. He is led right up to the edge of a cliff. The Teacher walks with him, and then says, 'Now jump off.' The pupil has taken many years to come to this point, this point of total abandonment, but it surely requires more than a little courage to take this great leap into the unknown. 'Don't worry,' says the Teacher. 'Sooner or later it had to come to this. Trust! Trust!'

The pupil stops for a moment, and then jumps. Sailing into the air he notices that there is a tree half-way down the cliff. Desperately he clings to it. He hears the branch cracking as a voice comes from above. 'Let go! I'll see you there.' The branch breaks. He falls way down into the cavern. The pupil is surprised to find that it is the softest landing in the world. He has landed in the arms of his Teacher, who has got there before him.

Energy of a certain type, refined and strong, has to be produced at the right time for the commitment to have any meaning at all. The energy must come, not from second-hand thought, but from the most creative aspect of ourselves. We need to settle down for a few moments, breathe consciously, and prepare ourselves to take a step into the unknown, for we may never see the total result of our actions. A true commitment is a commitment that is made *outside* of time as we know it. It has to be unconditional. It has to be strong, and it needs fertile ground for the result of that commitment to take root.

The paradox to all this is that although we can have a certain control over time, we cannot necessarily say when the ground will be ready to receive the seeds that are sown. Perhaps we have a great idea which we, as

agents for the idea as it were, realise is vitally important
for our time, and yet there is no one else ready to receive
the idea. The idea then goes into the world of possibilities,
a sort of Divine filing system, so to speak, and the world
has to wait until someone else can see the obvious need
for something to happen for the benefit of all mankind.
The knowledge of the 'Triad of freedom' can also produce
a loneliness, but it is a creative loneliness, a feeling deep
within the heart that all is well. As Julian of Norwich said,
'All will be well again, I know . . .'.

Without commitment there is hesitancy and then
there is wastage of time. Again that means that thought
is dangling over possibility, blocking out the light that
is needed for real growth to take place. We need to be
prepared to make an unconditional commitment and, of
course, the absolute commitment is to life itself. It is at
that moment that there is the only true freedom.

We need to ask ourselves, before undertaking
anything, whether we are actually *willing* to pay the price
of commitment. Are we actually willing to go through
what is sometimes called 'intentional suffering' in order
that the original commitment to an ideal or an idea can
work itself through into our world?

Even what may seem to be a very small decision can
affect thousands of lives. We all know this. Surely we
need to remind ourselves continuously that it is freedom
that we all look for; freedom *from* illusion and unnecessary
suffering, freedom *in* knowledge, and freedom *for* our
children and our children's children. For this to happen
every real dream or vision that is as yet unfulfilled has to
be fulfilled, just as every bad thought built from anger,
resentment, envy, greed and so on needs to be turned
back from the darkness into light.

Every single time that we commit ourselves, totally
and unconditionally, to even the smallest decision, there
is something that starts to move in the higher worlds
to come and help us. Something changes for good.
Unredeemed thought moves backwards through time to
its origin. The simplest acts made by the humblest people
in the world can have just as great an effect as the endless

meetings of so many good-willed people where there is
no real commitment, no agreement and no willingness to
pay the price of decision.

There is a beautiful and true story about how one
humble man's efforts made a total change in a certain
area of France. He was called 'the Man of the Trees' and
a little book was written about him which is called *The
Man who Planted Hope and Grew Happiness*.

The story took place at the time of the First World War.
The man was discovered quietly and silently planting oak
trees. All by himself, with no help, he was growing trees
in an area which was dry and neglected. The few people
who lived there were raw, violent and seldom spoke to
each other. The wind was hot and relentless. Yet this
man knew, in some way or another, that he could bring
about great change just by continuing to plant the trees
he raised from the seeds that he gathered.

At the end of the war, the man who originally found
him returned to see if the tree-planter was still alive.
Indeed he was! He had moved on from oak trees to
beech trees and others. A veritable forest had grown up.
What is more, streams were running where there had
been no streams before. The pastures were green and
people were moving into the area to farm. Children were
smiling and happy. There had been a complete transformation. Eventually the government recognised what he
had done. Elzeard Bouffier died peacefully in 1947. One
man's humility, perseverance and commitment changed
a whole area of a country. His story has spread around
the world, bringing hope to all who read the book.

'Am I willing?' 'Am I committed?' 'Am I in agreement?'
If we can say yes to these three questions we immediately
put ourselves into the path of service and therefore begin
to move away from the tyranny of time as we have
previously known it. Time is now on our side, and in the
words of famous Sufi mystic, 'Many strange things will
happen; ask God to inform you.'

10

EXPECTATION

*'There is always a mirror in the moment. We
can always face ourselves in the mirror with
the right question.'*

When we look at the 'Triad of Freedom' we are talking
about the potential freedom of the soul. It is said that
the soul is a knowing substance and its natural heritage is being free from the limitations of this world, the
limitations of time, gravity and so on. It is the freedom
that exists in actually being here on the planet in the
knowledge of oneself and of the true continuity of the
Life that never dies. Total commitment to life itself leads
us to this freedom. We can be told this so many times, and
given endless pieces of knowledge about it, but it is our
own personal responsibility to take the knowledge from a
world of theory and put it into action right down here in
the relative world. Transcendence without immanence
only opens one wing of the soul.

There is freedom 'from'; there is freedom 'in' and
there is freedom 'for'. There is freedom from the illusion
that we are separate from the Unity; there is freedom in
self-knowledge, and thus there is freedom for our children
and our children's children. Just as 'the Life' can never
die, so the Breath, now seen as the Spirit of God, can
never die. It is one long continuity, both permeating
and inter-penetrating the relative world, and yet standing
above it *at the same time.* It is permanent in the eternal
present and it adapts itself in the relative world through
the tides of breathing of a human being.

The obvious key to understanding any of these matters
is complete honesty. If we are truly honest with ourselves
we know that most of the time we are not totally awake

to the present moment, and thus, once again, we are in separation. The moment we are honest we find that we want to wake up. We want to be in the present moment more than anything else. There are even moments when we get glimpses of this real world, this life-line of continuity of which we are part. Each of these waking moments is like a bead on a rosary that we are continuously threading in our efforts towards consciousness until one day the rosary will be complete and there will be no separation. Each of the beads is a necessary part of the rosary itself, sealed with the knot of eternity.

Once we accept that honesty will help us to wake up, the next step is to look at our own attitude to life itself. There is no better way of doing this than just to stop for a moment, sit still and breathe! We can contemplate on continuity by watching the rise and fall of our own breathing, and noticing how often we are far from the beautiful feeling of harmony, that sound of inner knowledge. After a while, still observing the breathing, we can come into the stillness and reaffirm our undertaking in the 'triad of freedom'. We can ask ourselves, in all honesty, whether we are indeed totally committed to life. If we are, then when the time is right, everything that stands between the beads on the rosary will, little by little, disappear. Honesty brings forth the flame that burns away the dross until there is real knowledge of the Unity whilst still living in the relative world. There are some people who see God in creation and there are others who see creation in God. Those who know see God in creation and creation in God *at the same time*.

It is essential to talk more about the subject of expectation as one of the pitfalls along the journey. In certain traditions it is called 'the Red Death' since the result of expectation produces endless delays on the road.

On the surface it is not difficult to understand the predicament in which we so often find ourselves – that is, of expecting something to happen, or expecting someone to behave just as we want them to or feel they ought to behave. The result of such stupidity is inevitably disappointment, even grief and resentment. What actually happens is that we continuously hide behind the three walls that separate us from Truth, the walls of resentment, envy and pride. These barriers need to be recognised, openly and honestly, by each one of us. Through expectation we cover the walls with our opinions and negative emotions until they can scarcely be seen. We cannot transform resentment, for instance, if we cannot see that we have some. However, dealing with the causes of expectation is not an easy matter at all. Much has to be looked at and examined and we need to dig deep to discover why each of us so often fails to halt the process that leads to expectation in good time.

First of all it might help if we realise that expecting something to be just the way that *we* want it to be is just plain bad manners! Since all gifts come from God, who are we to stand in the way of Divine Harmony? Of course, since we are given a certain degree of free will, we can, and often do, interrupt what is intended. But this delays the process of our own transformation as well as that of others. We are all interconnected and this needs to be continuously remembered and brought to mind.

Expectation is a projection of our own desires. There is another danger of the path which is also connected to the causes underlying the disease of expectation. This danger is to do with what is so often termed 'Channelling'. Channelling is a form of mediumship whereby someone feels that he or she is in direct contact with some sort of entity in the invisible worlds, normally having lived in another epoch, who is using that person to bring forth what the entity feels needs to be said. It is interesting to note that the emergence of such phenomena always appears towards the end of a cycle when there is great fear about letting go of the past. As I said, this also coincides with a period of wars and natural disasters. Just now there is a whole rush of these people channelling everything from discarnate American Indians to Tibetan 'Ascended' Masters and Egyptian priests. Surely anyone with the slightest sense of discrimination would stop, breathe and listen before becoming involved with what is mainly just a rather pathetic form of quackery. Of course there are exceptions.

It is important that we do approach such matters seriously indeed, but also armed with the sword of a sense of humour. One evening in Germany I was giving a lecture with my translator by my side. I had been speaking on this very subject when a woman stood up in the audience and said, 'I am told that Atlantis is sending out an SOS!' 'Really, madam?' I replied. 'But I have heard from the highest source that Atlantis was wiped out by syphillis.' The translator, not quite understanding my words, turned around to me in front of the very large audience and asked, 'Who?'

Humour is an art, a protection and a gift. Surely we need to have a sense of humour when it comes to such subjects. Recently we were talking to a famous healer about this. She laughed and laughed and said that she, personally, had met twenty-six different people in one year who had announced that they were told by a channel that they were the reincarnation of the Virgin Mary.

On a more serious note, I wonder how many people have questioned whether the so-called entity was fully realised when inhabiting this planet? People are so starved of knowledge that they literally conjure up these situations, fully expecting that they are going to get the answer to life without making any effort on their own part. They listen to what these channels tell them, which is normally either a forecast about the imminence of Armageddon, or else encouragement to be ready for spacecraft which are about to land at any minute and take them to a world full of milk and honey.

And, how many people have noticed that the person channelling, in a semi-state of trance, loses all sense of the breath. They are asleep to the moment, and therefore cannot be said to be conscious. If they are not conscious then they have slipped off the everlasting continuity of Love, falling back into a miserable world of false hope based on their own expectation of someone 'out there' who is going to make it all work for them.

This is dangerous stuff indeed, dangerous, that is, if we want to come to understand our true nature. As long as there is channelling, there is duality. There is the person who is doing the 'channelling' and there is this 'other' being who is trying to communicate to us poor mortals. If these entities, which are nothing more or less than bundles of unredeemed thought-forms, were not fully realised on earth, then how can they communicate the Knowledge of Unity? This world is a hunting ground for knowledge. This life is the only one we have, and the only chance of having dominion over ourselves, that is, our lower nature, or animal self. We are foolish indeed if we do not make good use of it, continuously reaffirming our commitment to life itself. We can so easily be led astray and then we have to find our way back to the true path once again.

The question will inevitably arise as to how we can sort out the true from the false, and whether there is any usefulness in some of the guidance that we are offered from 'other worlds'. It is true that there have been occasions when some most extraordinary revelations have been given and even prophecies that have come true. However, if we are honest with ourselves, a very minute portion of all the verbiage has been proven useful. Sometimes, for example, there has been a modern prophet who has produced some useful information, but, at the same time, he or she has also produced seemingly endless rubbish. If we had believed all that people have forecast, for instance, California would have already slid into the ocean!

How then can we 'test the spirits' as we are asked to do in the Bible? Who or what are the false prophets? I am asked this question again and again, and I always try to explain in the simplest possible way. I tell those who ask me whether so and so is a real spiritual master, or whether some guidance or other is valid, that since the Truth itself lies within each individual, albeit very veiled, we need only to search honestly and diligently within to find the answer. We need to come to that beautiful point of stillness, watch the breathing, and ask deeply for the answer. If we are really strong in our questioning, putting every ounce of passion into the question itself, we can sense whether this person or a certain situation rings true or not.

It is like a tuning fork. If you have a tuning fork of the note 'A' in one corner of the room, and you have another tuning fork of the same note also in the room, when you strike one of the tuning forks, the other will resonate in sympathy with the one struck. If, on the other hand, one of the forks is tuned to another note, then there will not be this sympathetic response. We have a right to demand the Truth. We must not be caught by the apparent glamour of prophecy. Truth prevails with an honest heart and our passionate desire to serve the Truth itself.

11

NOT THIS, NOT THAT!

*'A story can be understood on many different
levels and a sense of humour helps!'*

'Time is the eternal attribute of God.' 'Once upon a
time.' 'Being on top of time.' All these are themes offering
a challenge and yet words are often veils over the Truth.
Thus it is necessary to look deeply within to find the
answers for ourselves. Words can sometimes be seen to
be like mirrors, the challenge and the question polishing
the mirror of our own hearts. We do not have to agree with
what we read. Far from it! Even to strongly disagree with
the words can produce a surge of creative tension if we
do not judge or get caught up in our opinionated mind,
based on notions of the past.

In nearly all the esoteric traditions, the schools of
wisdom and learning that have continued through aeons
of time, the first step into the unknown is one of denial. In
Japanese it is said, 'Neti. Neti' – Not this. Not that. In the
Sufi Tradition they say, 'Lā ilāha illā' Llāh'. Lā means 'No'.
No, we cannot accept that this world of appearances and
suffering is all there is to life. We cannot accept that it
is possible to be filled with the Spirit, with Divine Grace,
until we are empty of ourselves and the opinions we
have of others. We will not accept greed and ignorance,
cruelty and willfulness, when it is not the Will of God. We
will not accept life without questioning its very nature.
We will not be ruled by ignorance when we are potentially
intelligent human beings. No. No. No. Lā ilāha (There is
no God) illā' Llāh (except God).

It is easy to encapsulate the ego in more and more
opinions through affirming how wonderful everything is,

whilst being blind to the real needs of the moment. It is not easy to work on ourselves so that there is nothing outside the present moment and thus there is only He, *Hū*, that miraculous sound that we have already talked about. We have to cut down the thorn bushes of judgement and opinion to find the rose that has been waiting for the light so that it can show its beauty to the world. We have to be ruthless with ourselves. No, I will *not* be subjected to my lower nature. No, I will not let that rose be covered again. I will strip away all unnecessary form. I will polish the mirror of the heart so, like the old man on the beach, others may see themselves in it. No, I do not want anything except union with the Divine. I do not want separation anymore.

From all this negation, we can then honestly cry out *Yes* to the world. Yes, I know that there is only One Absolute Being. Yes, I know that it is we, human beings, who are the Saviours of God. It is we, who, through loving recognition, can free the imprisoned God within so that the soul can fly again, like the dove carrying the olive branch across the ocean after the Flood.

It is through the balance of denial and affirmation that, little by little, we break down the walls of form that bind us. In the end, all form has to go, and yet we are given this physical vehicle in which we live during our lifetime. Life is a seemingly endless paradox. We need the form in order to live on planet Earth, since we are the custodians of our planet. And yet, what is often called 'the real world' is not limited by the physical laws of the universe alone. To understand our essential unity we are given this lifetime as a gift and a perfect opportunity to come to true realisation. When we are free of all opinions, and our seeing and our hearing are not clouded by the results of our own judgements, we can truly be in the world and yet not of the world. We stand in this world but bow in the next – all at the same time!

There is a wonderful story to illustrate the breaking of form. I have read it in many different versions from various religious traditions. Like all true stories, it can be understood on at least seven levels if we question the inner meaning and see why the story is given to us at certain times and not at others.

One day the Imam of a famous mosque (the Imam is the one who leads the prayers and teaches the Koran) was approached by a friend. He told the Imam that he had some serious information that he should know. 'Come with me,' said the Imam and they walked off into the grounds of the mosque and sat near to the fountain where the faithful wash before entering for the daily prayers. 'There is some trouble?' he asked. Gravely the man leaned forward, looking around to see if anyone was listening. 'Imam,' he began, 'you know that little island just at the mouth of the river? A few of us have been listening very carefully in the evening when it is quiet, and it seems that there is a man out there who perhaps has prayed just a little too much.'

'But what do you mean?' asked the Imam. 'How can the faithful pray too much?' 'Well, you see,' said the man. 'He has got the prayer backwards, the wrong way round. Possibly he has gone a little too far and needs some help. You see, Imam, you taught us to say, 'Lā ilāha illā Llāh', Muhammadur Rasulu' Llah (There is no God but God and Muhammad is His Prophet), and later 'Allah Hū (God, He). Now this man way out there on the island can be quite clearly heard saying, 'Hū Allah' and not 'Allah Hū'. And he goes on all day and most of the night. I felt I just had to tell you. Of course I did not want to interfere.'

The Imam brightened up. His day had been made! Now he could do a good deed and help Allah in His Work. Of course he should go across to the island and put this man to rights. Obviously he was one of the faithful, but must have been out there on the island for too long. He had not attended the mosque on Fridays, otherwise he would know better than to get the prayer the wrong way round. Perhaps he had even gone a little mad. The Imam knew that these things can happen if people pray too much and forget the world. He would take action at once.

'Go and find me a boat, my good man,' said the Imam, standing up authoritively. 'I will go and attend to this matter. You did well to come and tell me. Heaven will reward you.' He patted the man on the head, saying a few prayers himself, and instructed that he was to be told the moment a boat had been found. Later in the day the man came running with the news that the boat was waiting for the Imam and also that there was a man to row him across to the island. 'But no,' said the Imam. 'I will row myself. This is work that should only be done by certain people.'

Smiling contentedly the Imam, in his robes and turban, bravely started rowing the boat across to the island. Unfortunately the wind started to get up. White caps dotted the water. The boat rocked and those watching on the shore were fingering their prayer beads with great speed. However, Allah was on his side, and the Imam, somewhat dampened from his experience, eventually reached the island. Pulling the boat up on the sand, he waved back at the others on the mainland. Listening carefully he could hear the sound of 'Hū Allah!', echoing across the island. 'Hū Allah!' 'Hū Allah!'

For a moment the Imam was spellbound. He remembered the sound of the wind in the trees and how his own beloved teacher had taught him that the sound Hū was the first manifested sound in the universe, bringing with it all the angels and archangels and the endless possibility from the Higher Worlds. He smiled, but then quickly remembered his mission. Picking up his robes so that they did not get soiled by the sand and the earth, he hastened in the direction of the sound.

Coming into a little glade in a wood, he saw the man. He was obviously a dervish, one of those strange people who have given their lives so totally to Allah that there is nothing left of the false personality. On the other hand, the Imam thought, the dervish could just have gone mad. He would call upon the Name of God and help.

Approaching carefully, he sat down near the man, whose eyes were closed. He coughed several times, first quietly and then louder. Soon the dervish looked around. Shocked that he had not noticed before, he jumped to his feet and bowed deeply. 'Forgive me,' he said. 'I was saying my prayers. I did not notice you come Imam. It is unforgivable. I am so sorry.'

'Do not worry, my friend,' said the Imam. 'God is the Only Friend. Hū dost! He will help. He has told me to come to see you since I was informed that you have given your life to God so totally that you have forgotten the correct way to say the prayer.' He smiled kindly, putting his arm on the dervish's shoulder. 'Of course it can happen to any of us. But you see, the words should be repeated like this: Allah Hū, Allah Hū and not Hū Allah!'

Tremendously relieved, the Imam wiped a tear from his eye. Allah had guided him to do this good deed for the day. All would be well! The dervish bowed even more deeply. 'Oh, thank you, thank you,' he said. 'It is true that I have been here a long time. Of course now I will repeat the words in the correct order. Oh, thank you. And I shall attend the mosque on Fridays once more.'

With that the Imam bade the dervish farewell and went back to his boat. The wind had abated somewhat but it was still very rough and the boat rocked dramatically. His friends were waiting on the other side, still saying their prayers for the safety of the Imam. But the Imam was pleased; the day had gone well. The rough water did not bother him. He was humming a little tune that he had learned as a child when suddenly, to his utter surprise, he saw the dervish walking across the top of the water towards him. 'Excuse me, Imam,' he said as he got close to the boat. 'What was it you said? I've forgotten . . .'

12

REINCARNATION AND ETERNAL RECURRENCE

*'When we make a total commitment, everything
that is needed in the play of life is given to us.
If the commitment is to and for life, then it is
possible for a human being to become complete
in one lifetime. Otherwise there are a series of
plays within the Great play, each one perhaps
a training ground for the final commitment,
which is both the final answer and then the
final question.'*

Many people say that I am liable to turn sacred cows
into hamburgers, but in no way do I attempt to destroy
anyone's belief systems. Rather I try to leave a valid set of
questions which will give you something to contemplate
upon. A Living School produces questions and challenges, and not merely answers. We all have to find out
what is real for each one of us. In this way we are links in
the chain of honesty.

Again and again the subject of reincarnation is
brought up in conversations concerning life, the purpose
of life, who and what we are and where we are going after
the death of this transient bodily existence. It is not useful
to feed answers, which at their very best can only be
second-hand. At the same time, I consider we have a right
to ask important questions such as the one concerning
reincarnation, and, even more, I feel it is almost our
obligation to ask such questions so that we, and others,
do not continue to live in a flat world of second-hand and
third-hand knowledge.

The subject of reincarnation is a delicate one and it is surely one of the sacred cows of the spiritual path these days. During the last fifty years it has become very fashionable to talk about reincarnation, almost as though there are experts who know, first-hand, what it is all about. We are asked to accept the notion that we reincarnate again and again, learning a little more with each lifetime, but seldom, if ever, do people question exactly what it is that reincarnates. When I challenge people with this question there is usually a brief silence and the shuffling of feet. I have even seen people become quite angry.

It is easy to fall into the trap of glamorising life and achieving a sense of self-importance when someone, for example, comes up to us and says, 'I knew you before. We were lovers in ancient Egypt but you died young and now we have met again in order to fulfil our dreams . . .' Honestly, such nonsense is spoken daily, mostly based on vain superstitions and sentimentality.

Reincarnation almost implies that there is a vast breeding ground for beings getting ready to incarnate. After all, the population of the world gets bigger and bigger! Do we have a strong enough being to move across space and time, perhaps jumping several hundred years? What did it do inbetween incarnations? We are told that we incarnate into a male body one time around and then a female body another time. Who is it that keeps a balance of the sexes? There are many explanations and mostly they contradict each other.

As I said, I am not denying people's visions and dreams, but it is surely a good thing to question, if reincarnation is part of someone's belief system, who or what is it that reincarnates? Is it a portion of our Being? Is it the soul, and if so, what *is* the soul? There are many definitions for the word 'soul' in the dictionary. I was taught that the soul is a 'Knowing substance'. What then is this substance and of what is it composed? Is it an element, or a composite of many elements? These are sensible questions.

In no way am I denying the individual. The individual is the witness of God, so beautifully explained in one of the sayings of the Prophet Muhammad (Peace and blessings) when it was said, as though by God, 'I was a hidden treasure, and I loved to be known, so I created the world that I might be known.' What a wonderful description of the play of life! Just as each individual is a unique aspect of the Unity, so no two thumbprints can ever be the same. The knowledge of Unity is a unique privilege given to each one of us when we search diligently for the Truth.

I am also not denying certain religious beliefs which include reincarnation as part of their doctrine. It is an Eastern concept and for some people maybe it is a way of coming into the Unity. However, we live in the West. We think completely differently. It could even be said that the geometry of the Western mind is different to that of its Eastern equivalent. Language and sound play such a huge part in our lives, and the very sound of the meaning of the word reincarnation in Sanskrit would make little sense to us unless we had generations of the Hindu tradition behind us. After all, sound fixes pattern, and at least a portion of our genetic structure is made from patterns created by the sounds lying within language.

We also need to understand that the concept of time in the East is totally different to that of the West. In the East, life is seen as a process of unfoldment. In the West we struggle to understand everything, or explain away that which we are not given to understand through vague concepts and copies of Eastern ideas. Our life is a rather abrupt expression of everlastingness. As the sun rises in the East, so true knowledge stems from the East. But it returns to the West. In other words, it comes again to the West where it also is, but seen from a different angle of the rays of the sun. As the sun moves across the face of the planet, the water rises up and drops again in the West. The breath, containing moisture distilled through the wisdom of the ages, breathes forth the waters of knowledge in a way that is acceptable to the West. It is said in the inner teachings that there will come a day when the East and the West will join in the knowledge of the One Brotherhood of Man in the Fatherhood of God, and there will be true and mutual understanding which will then be offered to the North. We cannot wait for this to happen all on its own. It is up to us to work towards this great vision.

I am not denying the idea of reincarnation. What I *am* saying is that from within and out of the Unity there is continuous unfoldment, with the One Principle of All eternally recurring in a myriad of ways until the end of time. The end of time is when we have reached beyond the fourth dimension whilst still inhabiting this body on planet Earth. When this transformation has been completed on all levels there is surely no need to have to repeat the same old lessons. There will be others to be learned but they will be more on a group consciousness level. At this stage we know of our own uniqueness within the Unity, and yet there is no sense of separation. We no longer think our way into separation on a daily basis since there is no further need to think about ourselves as such. Life takes on a completely different meaning, new and fresh. This world of illusion has been turned into the stage of life itself.

'All right,' says mind. 'We are here so presumably we have come from somewhere and therefore we are going somewhere. We cannot come out of nowhere and return to nowhere. That cannot be in the Divine Plan. Anyway, how could I have a distant memory of things that have happened in past time, and even in past epochs, if I had not already been there?'

Mind asks many questions like this. Mind wants explanation in comparison for that is its only food. Mind has to believe in its own existence, almost as if separate from the Whole. Little mind tells us to believe in reincarnation because little mind does not want to be assimilated into bigger mind and finally Universal Mind. Little mind says 'You' and 'Me', but never 'O Thou', addressing the God in each one of us. Little mind lives in temporal time and wants to continue the illusion of mind's separate existence. Thus little mind will, in a sense, reincarnate. Little mind tells us that there is something that was having a wonderful time as a nobleman in Paris during the early part of the eighteenth century, but little mind cannot say what it was that was the noble-man.

Supposing that, in reality, we did not come from anywhere, and that there is nowhere to go, except to actually get *here*, perhaps the most difficult task that any human being could ever be given in this lifetime. How can we come to this realisation? Is it not through the very Breath itself? We come into this world on the breath and we go out on the breath. What lies in between these two breaths is our very precious life-span, for some of us the only life we have to come to true self-realisation. 'Know thyself', it is asked of us. It is through the breath that the necessary transformation takes place to release the soul, that hidden knowledge, from the dark recesses of the cave of illusion. The soul is a 'Knowing substance'. Deep within it knows, but like the Sleeping Princess in all the legends, it has to be awakened so that God's wisdom can be made manifest on Earth.

What is this substance, this substance of the soul that can provide the wings with which to fly home? Perhaps it is made up of myriads of little minds who have given up their sense of separation to make one pure, unadulterated soul, lying in the bosom of the One Soul. In the sacred documents we read that the body is the Virgin Mary and there is a Jesus within each of us, but if our yearning is not sufficient then Jesus will return back along the secret path from whence he came.

In the words of Mevlana Jelaluddin Rumi:

> *I died as a mineral to become a plant.*
> *I died as a plant to become an animal.*
> *I died as an animal to become Man.*
> *I will die as man to rise in angel form.*
> *On, on shall I go.*

This world is a theatre and we are the players. How many times we have been told that! God created the play, the stage, the actors and the actresses. He created one great plot, and gave us the creation story verbatim in less time than the opening and closing of an eye. He said *Kun* ('Be!') and the play was set in motion. From the one play come many plays since He likes to see what He has created, but He does not like to see His play limited by vain repetition. Once the play is learned, He wants us to move on to bigger and better things. He wants us to move to the theatre in the Heavens. This world is a transitory world. It is a world of appearances. It is a world of suffering because the rose-bush needs to be pruned in order that there is a perfect rose and the heart is finally opened.

If the breath is in true balance, what need is there for reincarnation? Rather we see the eternal recurrence of the Divine Principle spread out in front of us, everything and everyone having its part to play. We are in the world but not of the world. We see the endless 'helpers' within the Unity of God, both visible and invisible. We are no more caught by the tyranny of time in the relative world nor limited by gravity, for the adventure that we call life spreads out in all directions at once, moved by the Breath of His Compassion.

13

THE SHEEP AND THE GOATS

*'The future of the world is dependent upon
love.'*

All the great religions have stressed that the universe
is made for man and not the other way around. God
made man in His image and so what is there that is not
within man? The voyage of exploration to the innermost
parts of the soul is an adventure indeed, and like any real
adventure, there is difficulty and there is potential danger.
Balance is necessary all along the way. Most surely we
can only go some of the way on our true life's journey
without the knowledge of breath, in which is contained
life itself. There will always be organic evolution, which
has gone on from the beginning of time, but conscious
evolution requires conscious human beings whose very
breath makes all the difference in the world.

Paradoxically it is the sacrifice of who and what
we *think* we are that produces the possibility of real
understanding. Normally when we think, we think relat-
ing everything to ourselves and thus causing more and
more separation. It is true that we are all unique examples
of the One Unity, but we are not separate. Everything
is interconnected. Try thinking without thinking about
yourself! There is a famous prayer which starts with the
words, 'Father, take away the "I am" that stands between
Thee and me.' It is this illusion of separation that has to
go so that we are indeed breathing alive, breathing life
itself and thus sharing consciously in this beautiful world.
When we can understand this very basic principle then
we are well on the way towards a new cycle of history.

At certain specific times of history tremendous possibilities are given to us to wake up to what is often

called 'The Real World', i.e. a world that is fresh and free with each moment, rather than a carry-over of yesterday's hangover of half-forgotten dreams. Unfortunately these opportunities also coincide with great dramas being played out on the face of the earth. Sometimes we have been faced with wars. Sometimes it is a series of natural disasters which beset us and famine and disease strike. It almost seems unfair and yet it is at these times that great strides can be taken in conscious evolution.

Just now we have many examples. There is indeed vast famine in our time. Acid rain is destroying our forests and polluting our rivers and lakes. The drinking water is contaminated with toxic waste, lead and mercury poisoning. Hundreds of thousands of bird and animal species are dying out. The dreaded disease of AIDS, often called this century's version of the Black Death, is sweeping through the Western world. Violence grows, riots are everywhere. At the same time, paradoxically, there are vast technological changes which we can scarcely keep up with.

It is as though we are being forced through a funnel into a totally new way of life from which there is no escape. It is not a pretty picture and yet it is a real picture. We cannot just ignore what we see and think that it is going to go away in the night. There is no way now that this can happen. Real change, and not merely the apparency of change, has to come about in our time if we are to survive at all. For this to happen we need to learn how not to identify with the situation or panic when the going gets tough. The first and most vital thing to realise is that we have to face the situation just as it is, without fear.

I remember when I was studying with the Druids. The Arch-Druid at that time was a wonderful old Scottish homoeopathic doctor, explosively wise at times, delivering ultimatums that were meant to shock us into the present moment. One day he turned to me and said that in my own lifetime I would witness such a dramatic change that the ancient biblical prophecy, the separation of the sheep from the goats, would unfold in front of my eyes. He went on to explain that it would almost be as though mankind would be divided into two distinct types.

Those that for one reason or other could not cope with the necessary changes would be left behind. He even forecast at that time that there would be disease and famine out of all proportion. I did not like what I was being told. I was very young and it was not long after the Second World War when we were all looking forward to a new world, a vision of hope, where true brotherhood and humanitarianism would prevail.

That wasn't so many years ago, and now, if we are honest with ourselves, we can see that the division has already taken place. What the doctor meant by this statement was that there are those who want to know, and there are those who do not want to know, being unable to face the changes necessary within themselves as well as in the outer world. There are still others, as yet asleep, who do indeed have tremendous possibilities and who will have to know for the good of the planet and its future.

It is not easy to face the vast changes that are necessary without fear. Perhaps there will always be some degree of it, since we are, after all, human, but when we start to wake up to the breath, so our attitude changes and that, in itself, is a big step in the right direction.

Someone who is truly in control of his or her breath is not only 'walking on air' but is then also on top of time in the relative world. He is no more swept along by the relative nature of time but rather time passes *through* him in its eternal aspect, just as the element of air passes through him, becoming transformed to help the world through the world of nature. In the same way, the world of nature helps in the process of organic evolution. Times takes on a different meaning altogether and the psychology of man is seen in an entirely different light. His behaviour patterns change and a whole new understanding emerges in his consciousness. When we are on top of the breath, and when the tides of breathing reflect the Divine Order, then we are functioning as human beings, no more controlled by the animal passions within us. They have been transformed to become useful friends working for us and not the other way around. Conscious evolution and organic evolution hold hands at last.

14

DESTINY

'Beyond listening is hearing. First you listen;
then you hear.'

Thus far I have given many challenges and now I would
like to offer some clear guidelines to help us on what is
called 'the Road of Truth'. I have frequently mentioned
the word *Sufi* and the Sufi Tradition, but even the beauty
within that tradition can turn into form which, too, has
to be broken down for the essence to be seen and understood. There are so many books on Sufism, and the stories
of the Sufi Masters and the Dervish Brotherhoods are too
numerous to mention. Countless numbers of seekers have
read books talking about the quest for knowledge and
have struggled to follow the same journey. I am sure that
if we are destined to meet up with these people it will
happen in one way or another.

The pilgrimage I made, as told in my first two books,
has drawn many along the route I took through Turkey,
visiting the holy shrines and cities. Not everyone found
the people I mentioned although the instructions as to
where the people lived were fairly explicit. The bookseller
in Istanbul was in fact a very famous Shaykh of one of the
Dervish Brotherhoods, and those that did meet him were
granted extraordinary hospitality. I did not give his name
for I knew that if it was right then the seekers would
find him in the same way they would find the Shaykh
of the Mevlevi Brotherhood in Konya. My own teacher,
whom I called Hamid, preferred to remain mostly in the
background, and so I gave neither his real name nor
where he lived. However, some people did find him but
that was more difficult and required much patience and

perseverance. After all, from reading the books, which were set mainly in Turkey and Mexico, they would hardly expect to find him living in the wilds of Scotland!

As I have said, it is *kismet* (Destiny) that draws us on, and it can even be said that the whole map of our lives is already written in that book. On the other hand, it does not mean to say that we will find the book, let alone open it and read what is inside. If we do, then we will see the signs laid out right in front of us. There will be pointers showing us the way and rules will be given to help us and protect us. Even if we do come upon the book that contains the story of our own destiny, that does not mean to say that we can just open it up and follow along the pages without making any efforts on our own part. Much effort indeed has to be made and we have to be well and truly awake, lest we lose our direction in what is merely a world of attraction. And yet, paradoxically, it is often attraction which starts us off in the first place but it is the breath which keeps us straight on the path.

With all the many alternatives being offered today in the name of Truth, it is hard for people to know which is destiny and which is fate. I always try to teach people to be consciously discriminating, honouring their own integrity and their lives which are so precious. In order to keep us straight, strange and difficult tasks are sometimes given. It is said that if we take one step towards God, then He will take ten steps towards us.

I was once invited to speak to a group of people in California, most of whom had read my books. During the lunch-break there was the usual crowd, waiting to ask the questions which they probably should have asked before. On that particular day there was no back exit and so I was pinned against the wall by some fierce-looking intellectuals who seemed to want to have all the answers by the end of the day, and were quite ready to blame me if they were not fully enlightened by that time.

One of these people had a large black beard and looked as though he might have been a Rabbi or perhaps a Greek Orthodox priest. In fact, it turned out he was neither – he taught psychology at the university. His particular interest was healing in its many aspects and since he had read my books, he had decided that I was definitely the person to approach. I felt he meant well despite his greedy attitude and over-ebullience and so I asked him to meet me after the day's class was over.

It is very important that a teacher never humbles or distresses an aspirant on the Path. At the same time it is necessary to know what could attract someone in the right direction. In this case, it was obvious to me that the gentleman had tremendous unawakened possibilities within him, but his mind and his heart were set on the subject of healing. Unfortunately, the very word can be like a branch line on the railway track, leading nowhere but to a dead end. Anyway, it was too good an opportunity to miss and so I ventured an opening for him.

'Have you got any money?' I asked. Again it was quite obvious that he was wealthy but that he needed to be honest about it. He acknowledged that he was not needy and then I went on to ask him if he could take a sabbatical for a few months. By chance he said that this was not only possible but it could be part of a thesis he was writing about the various types of healing used in the world, if indeed I could give him any contacts.

We were sitting in the patio of a little restaurant in Berkeley. The moment was so intense that people were staring in our direction. I was careful not to speak too loudly. My proposition to him did sound a little like some sort of spiritual espionage!

'You need to learn Spanish,' I said, 'because I want to send you to an extraordinary healer, who is most particularly a herbalist, and he does not speak any English. You don't need to speak the language fluently, but it is important, in all respect to him, to be able to express your needs. Of course I'm sure that there will be people who can translate.'

'When do I go?' he asked. You could see his eagerness vibrating in every part of him.

'But wait,' I replied. 'That is only the start of the journey. But I don't want you to talk to people about all of these things. It is good that you keep things to yourself, otherwise the wrong people might want to come with you and then everything could be wasted.'

'Go to Tepotzlan first,' I said, and I wrote down an address for him and drew a little map on a piece of paper. I then went on to tell him that there was a small group of students still living in the area who would help him. 'You will be well received but I have told the study group that they have to keep a very low key and do their best not to be noticed. The local healers and magicians do not like the gringos and the tourists who have little or no respect for the people and their ancient traditions.'

Our friend was writing voluminous notes, as I continued with my instruction. It was a good day. I could feel that things were going to work out for him.

'The next thing for you to do, having met with my friends and got yourself adjusted to the different vibrations in such a place, is to go to Oaxaca. You can get there by bus with no difficulty and of course you understand that it is best to travel light. Carry a few clothes, plenty of water-purifying tablets and perhaps some snake-bite serum. You never know what you are going to meet up with.

'In Oaxaca there is a Shaman who is an expert on herbs. He was taught by a master. The knowledge has been handed down from generation to generation. It is possible that you will learn something there that can be useful back here in the States. There will be nine pupils studying with him, and I believe that two of them are from the States.'

His notebook was filling up. The light was going and waiters were lighting candles on the tables. 'Now don't stay too long with him,' I said. 'You will easily find out what is useful, and of course there can always be another chance for you to go back and learn more at another time. The healing arts are just another gift of God, but it is true knowledge that anchors Love. That is our job. You are looking for true knowledge, aren't you?' I asked him.

'Oh, most certainly,' he said.

'When you have learned all that you can, I want you to go to the Bolivian side of Lake Titicaca.' I went on to explain that way up in the mountains, on that side of the lake, there was a monastery that was a Centre for the Great White Brotherhood, an esoteric society that has existed at least as far back as the sixteenth century. The knowledge within the school has been handed down by word of mouth throughout the ages.

'You will also be received,' I told him, 'but not until those who live there are completely certain that your search is honest and pure and that what you need and want is nothing but the knowledge of the eternal Truth. You need to go well prepared and most important, practise the method of breathing that I have introduced today. Keep the rhythm going with every step you take on the journey. Breathe when you are walking; breathe when you are talking. It is possible you know. Breathe the rhythm before you go to sleep at night. Wake up breathing consciously. Remember that Breath *is* life. Do not go to sleep for one moment, and then you will be received.'

We shared some wine together as the first guests came in for the evening meal. The stars were out. There was a certain magic in the air. I imagine, that, for him, it was difficult to know what was real and what was not real at that time. Anyway, we shook hands in agreement and I asked him to write to me when he returned from his journey.

It was many months later until I heard from him. When the news came, it was good. Yes, he had gone to Tepotzlan. There he had met up with my friends, learned as much Spanish as he could and then went on to Oaxaca where he found the herbalist healer with his nine pupils. It is not difficult to find such a person if your intention is strong and pure! There were two pupils from the States and he did learn something about the healing arts that he could put to good use. He realised that it was indeed knowledge, true knowledge, that he wanted most in the world and he continued his journey. Many planes, trains and buses later he found the monastery in Bolivia. It was just as I had said.

The fact of the matter remains that I had never been to Oaxaca, nor had I known of a Shaman herbalist there, let alone met two American pupils. I had never been further south than Tepotzlan in my life, and had never seen Lake Titicaca.

So how could all this have happened? How was it possible to know about these people and places when I had never been there? Of course there are a hundred and one explanations, stretching from a belief in reincarnation, which would imply that I had been to Oaxaca and Lake Titicaca in a previous lifetime, to merely the psychic ability I had at the time of meeting the man. We all know that certain people have these gifts, but there may be another way of explaining the story which is better suited to the Western mind.

It is indeed possible to develop our own inner senses and then, just as the breath is not limited by time and space, so if something exists somewhere in the world, we can see and experience what is there. A great deal is to do with our attitude and whether we consider that these things are possible. We say that God is the only true guide and therefore, if the man was not sincere and was not predisposed to find what was already there, he would not have found it, even if I knew it existed. If he had not been honest in his search, perhaps suffering from personal greed, he would have been led astray. If he had not persevered, he would have faltered. As it was he put himself into the arms of Destiny and was guided all the way.

The story came true, probably because the man needed the experience to give him the necessary confidence to keep straight in his search for Truth. The actual journey itself was not that important. It was the testing of his ability to trust completely that really counted. I imagine it would have been hard to return to the opinionated, intellectual world in which he was raised. I pray, instead, that he will have started on the journey to his spiritual home.

15

SENSIBILITY

*'Inside ourselves we have that same belt, which
acts as a protection from too much light/
realisation at once. In the process of
transformation, little by little, this begins to
melt. And then we find that this radiation that
was initially harmful can become useful.'*

The possibilities for man and woman are endless. In
the past fifty years there has been a quantum leap in
evolution and yet many people are simply not able to cope
with the changes. We could say that their spiritual and
psychic bodies are not adjusted to the speed of change.
They cannot absorb and digest that which is useful
for them. Without proper knowledge and the necessary
tools, certain types of energy can become increasingly
dangerous to us. The breakdown of the immune system
that we have seen in AIDS is just one example. All over
the world there is a similar breakdown of order. Without
sufficient training in what is sometimes termed 'the reciprocal maintenance of the planet', it is even possible that
early death will become more and more widespread over
the next twenty years. It is a frightening prospect and yet
one which offers a tremendous challenge.

We have been told so often that man is mainly asleep,
that is, asleep to his true nature. He can function with just
the use of the five senses, the senses of taste, touch, smell,
hearing and sight. He can manage, that is, until some sort
of crisis that is incomprehensible to the normal senses
occurs. Then he is lost. He cannot cope. He is out of his
depth.

Surely this is just such a time. We are hanging onto
the past like grim death, too fearful to give up outdated
and outmoded political and social mores, and unable to
take that great big and wonderful step into the Unknown.

Time is not on our side. For those who live only in and for the senses, it is running out fast.

So what can be done? The astrologers' consulting rooms are filled with seekers begging for advice. Psychic fortune-tellers draw patterns in the sands of time, either forecasting doom and destruction or entirely the opposite. More and more people are relying on outer advice for help and yet the onus of responsibility surely should be put back onto the individuals themselves.

I always tell people that whatever they learn should be able to be put into everyday use, right down here on earth. The practices I teach are not designed to get us into a transcendental state, a half-way house between thinking and being. Far from it. Life itself is the true school and life wants us *here*. When we do finally get here we discover that there is nowhere else. When we are truly here then we have somewhere from which to expand our consciousness. To try to reach out from the very thin thread of consciousness that we have in our underdeveloped state is indeed foolhardy and can lead to madness and even death, not the death of the false ego but the death of possibility.

We come back to the nature of breath once again. The more we are awake to the breath, in all its wonder and beauty, the more we learn balance and the more we have the ability to remain rooted in the earth, whilst being able to soar to unimaginable heights of realisation, without leaving the room in which we are. Without the knowledge of breath, all the practices that are given inevitably will remain, at best, second-hand experiences. We can breathe with someone. We can breathe with a group of like-minded people. We can breathe for someone in distress, such as in the dying process, in order to give them confidence. Ultimately the responsibility of actually breathing consciously remains with each individual alone. It is we, as individuals, who are asked to attune ourselves to the Divine rhythm and harmony pervading and inter-penetrating the universe.

I believe that the first step towards living in a higher level of being is to make the five senses our friends. As we have heard so many times, we are mainly controlled by the senses. We do not work with them consciously, and yet they can be trained to be watch-dogs, acting as a protection in everyday life. But they have to be trained carefully. Some people have naturally developed senses, or perhaps one or more of them is very highly tuned. One person has a developed sense of smell, for example, and another's ability to hear sounds that most people cannot can be phenomenal. A blind man's sense of touch is acute to compensate for his lack of sight. Someone who is deaf may well be able to increase the sensitivity of the other senses. We take too much for granted. The senses are indeed our friends and will respond by being recognised like any domestic animal.

Try an experiment yourselves. Take one of the five senses on each consecutive day and work with it. Imagine that this is going to be the first time that you have done this consciously *all day*. It is not difficult and it is very rewarding. With practice you will find life much brighter and considerably more interesting.

Supposing you choose the sense of touch. The first thing to do is to agree the night before that this is what you are going to do the next day. The aim is to communicate with this sense of touch that you have and to let it know that you love it and need it. Next, find a small object that you can carry with you throughout the following day. It could be a favourite pebble or crystal formation. The Victorians used to make things called 'feelies'. These were normally made out of wood and would be small enough to fit into the palm of the hand. They were just nice, friendly objects and you would carry one around with you, feeling its contours, turning it over in your hand, giving it love.

It does not take very long before the hands become much more sensitive and they respond to this sense of touch and the object itself starts to take on a special quality, seemingly almost on its own. Over a period of time it is possible to sensitise a bowl full of such objects. Guests will orientate themselves towards it because of the energy that has been imparted. The hands are the extension of the heart and so, with the right effort and intention, the increased sensitivity and consciousness of the breath, the objects become special indeed.

In the evening before the experiment, choose your object and place it where it can easily be found in the morning. The next day when you have woken up, sit down for a few minutes and examine it. Turn it over in your hand; feel all the contours. Because each finger is different, feel it with each finger in turn, and then with all the fingers and finally the hand. Try to keep in the rhythm of the breath and also be awake to the room in which you are sitting.

Remember breath is not one of the five natural senses and yet, it is through the breath that the senses can receive correct food so that no more do they have dominion over us but rather they work with us on this journey we call life. In order to train the senses it is vitally important that we do not identify with them. When this happens, the object of the experiment is totally lost. They are our friends and want to help us.

When you have got used to the object, put it in your pocket or purse, knowing that you can always go back to feeling it on the bus or in the train on the way to work. You can carry it in your hand as you are walking. When you get to your office or place of work, you can pick it up whenever there is an opportunity. Watch the breath, breathe the rhythm and make that sense of touch your friend!

It is similar with the other senses. The following day you could choose the sense of taste. Taste the difference in everything you eat and drink. One lettuce may look the same as another but they may not taste the same. Perhaps one of them was grown on one farm, and another miles away where the minerals in the earth were different. Champagne is called champagne because it comes from that region in France. It cannot come from anywhere else. Sparkling wine can be made by employing the method used in the region of champagne but it can never be the real thing. The roots of the vines there have grown deep to taste the water, already carrying the natural minerals in the earth.

If you want to develop a sense of taste, watch a wine-taster. He rolls that wine around his mouth, activating the taste-buds and it almost looks as though he is chewing it! As he, little by little, develops his sense of taste, so he moves up the ladder of his profession. He has succeeded in making the sense of taste his valuable friend and ally.

We use our sense of smell in so many ways that it might be hard to see how to develop it. However, more and more we are understanding the value of this particular sense. For example, we now have what is called Aromatherapy, which is becoming very popular. It has been discovered that certain smells and perfumes can bring beneficial results and can even bring back distant and long-forgotten memories out of the subconscious, where they may have remained for half a lifetime.

We breathe automatically if we want to smell something but try smelling when you are conscious of the breath at the same time. The sense is immediately increased, responding to that heightened awareness. Once again, we are training the sense, not merely taking it for granted. These senses can even save our lives if we are awake. Certainly there would be a lot less food-poisoning if the packers and preparers knew when food was contaminated or not quite fresh. People in supermarkets could send out their senses to provide a knowledgeable report as to the state of the produce. With a bit of right effort, we could help the world to wake up.

To develop sight and hearing, again we need to remain conscious of the breath. Try looking and hearing *through* your eyes and ears and not from them. Remember that these are the eyes through which God sees and these are the ears through which He hears. If we could spend a whole day just looking through our eyes, a new world of possibility could be opened up to us, a world of countless dimensions that had not been perceived before. We need to be reminded. It is the same with hearing. Without listening, we will not be able to hear the sacred sound of *Hū*, the first manifested sound of the universe.

When you have worked with one sense a day, then practise working with two senses and more. It is necessary to continue working conscientiously until one day they all work together simultaneously. It is such a simple practice but surely many things would change in the world if every child knew how to make the senses their friends.

16

As Above, So Below

'A perfect rose only blooms in order.'

Today, with so many books written on new approaches to physics and the esoteric path in general, more and more people have at least heard of the *chakras*, the invisible subtle centres that interpenetrate the physical body. Translated from the Sanskrit language, *chakra* literally means 'wheel'. Throughout the East, these subtle centres are recognised. They have also been known in the Western mystical tradition but the knowledge has been hidden in symbols for the few who were educated in such matters. The vast majority of people were ignorant concerning these subjects, which were the sacred and secret possession of the priesthood.

To study the chakras in depth is a vast undertaking and is not the major focus of this book. I mention them only because we need to look at the subtle anatomy of man, at least in symbolic terms, when we come to the nature of breath. There is an immense amount of material available for anyone who wishes to pursue the subject.

I 'saw' or sensed the presence of these seven major subtle centres when I was very young. I had been taught the basics of conscious breathing when I was only five years old and feel that this most likely opened up certain inner channels within myself, thus increasing my own sensitivity to these matters. As a young child it all seemed perfectly natural, but it was also a lonely state of awareness. The way we see things in the invisible worlds is undoubtedly personal, although there are certain archetypal pictures of angels, fairies and the 'little people' that are more generally accepted. I would point out what I could see to older people and they would just discard my ideas as a child's vivid imagination.

Having no previous knowledge of the chakras, I did not perceive them in symbolic terms. In the East they are often illustrated as being like lotus flowers, each one seen as having a different number of petals. At that age, having read no books on the subject, I saw them looking rather like the jellyfish I had seen in the ocean on my holidays! I sensed them as being like vortices of energy, continuously in movement. It seemed as though they were taking in some form of energy and then sending it out again in certain directions, in a subtly different form, much in the same way as a jellyfish propels itself by taking in water, digesting the minute crustacea and swimming creatures, and then pushing it out again. I could see these subtle centres, each one interconnected, working with different vibrations and levels of energy.

The human being is a highly complicated transformer of subtle energies, taking in energies from higher sources and making them available to us. Many of these higher energies would be too strong for us in our ordinary state of existence and so the chakras act as natural filters for our own protection, at the same time affording us the energies that we need to play our part in the reciprocal maintenance of the planet. The chakras also take in the etheric counterparts of the mineral and the vegetable kingdoms. It is through them that colour irradiates our whole being. A total alchemical process is taking place.

Man stands as the bridge between heaven and earth. 'As above, so below.' Since the universe is made for human beings, we could even say that without us there would be no evolution beyond the level of the animal. And yet we know that the evolutionary process is continuing. It cannot happen without us and so again we look to the correct ways of breathing to keep all these subtle centres and channels open and functioning correctly.

Organic evolution passes through man in an upward and forward moving spiral, whereas conscious evolution comes from completion at the end of time, with the direct purpose of bringing the higher worlds right down here on

earth. As in the analogy of the passing trains, the higher
worlds wait to fulfil their own unique purpose when the
time is right. We are the suitable vessels in which the
necessary transformation can take place.

Many of these things can be seen illustrated in the
great stories and legends of all time. There have always
been sacred dances which have direct purpose as well as
symbolic meaning. Jesus said, when he had commanded
the disciples to make a circle, holding each other's hands,
and he standing in the middle: 'Now answer thou unto my
dancing. Behold thyself in me who speak, and seeing what
I do, keep silence about my mysteries . . . The number
twelve danceth on high. The whole of high hath part in
our dancing. Who so danceth not, knoweth not what
cometh to pass.'

Obviously Jesus knew of the mysteries as do the
dervishes of the Middle East. The word 'dervish' literally
means 'threshold' and he or she represents an active
bridge, a connection between these two aspects of the
evolutionary process. When he turns in his ecstatic
dance, he turns anticlockwise, bringing the higher energies to work for us. At the same time (since in reality
everything is unfolding from the still point in a turning
world) in his testimony to the Unity, as he calls on God's
Holy Name, a double vortex is set up within him. Finally
everything is perfectly blended in the heart. Each of the
subtle centres, the chakras, are now working in perfect
harmony. The channels are opened and so the refined
energy, blended in the alchemical marriage, is made
available on earth. Just as the breath is not limited by walls,
so, for the dervish who is said to be 'non-existent', there is
no limitation at all. He is both in the world, and yet not of
the world. He no longer needs the protection of filters to
veil the beauty of the pure Light of God. All has become
One again.

Perhaps you can now see that the inner meaning of the
sacred dance and its symbology has never really died out.
It was known at the time of Jesus and it was known at the
time of the Prophet Muhammad (Peace and Blessings . . .)
and his nephew Ali, from whose influence sprang the

major Dervish Brotherhoods. I used to wonder how much of 'the Dance' had been lost in the Christian Orders until one day a great friend of mine told me the story of what had happened to him when he was visiting the Chapel at Ephesus, the place where the Virgin Mary went after the Crucifixion.

There are nearly always many pilgrims at Ephesus. They have made the long 6 km climb up the mountain from the ancient ruins below, or have come in bus-loads from all over the world. I once saw a Mass celebrated in the open air outside the chapel because there were so many people that they could not get inside the building.

On this occasion, however, there was absolutely no one about. My friend sat quietly in prayer before lighting one of the candles for his family and friends. Looking around to be sure that he was alone, he started doing the Turn of the Dervishes. He was not from the Middle East but from Canada, and had been introduced into one of the Brotherhoods. With his arms raised way up above his head, the right hand lifted in the receptive position to be open to the energies from above, and with his left hand pointing to the ground so that the transformed energies would be brought to earth, he slowly started turning. The *Hū* was on his breath and the Name of God in his heart.

I would have loved to have seen his face when a priest appeared from a little adjoining chapel. Smiling in friendship, the priest put his fingers to his lips. 'Where did you learn the Turn?' he whispered. 'When no one is here I do the Turn too.'

17

WHO IS LOOKING?

*'Meditation is not drifting along in the furrows
of the mind. Meditation is an example of pure
discipline which can lead to the
contemplation of God.'*

Just as there are subtle 'wheels' turning and transforming
different aspects of energy, so, in this beautifully complex
structure of ours, there are gateways which can open us
to further realms of possibility. By opening these gates
we can start to develop the higher senses that are indeed
available to us once we have made the five lower senses
our friends and allies.

We can, little by little, develop clairvoyance which
is the art of seeing or sensing things as they actually are
and not only as they appear to be. It is the same with
clairaudience, i.e. the ability to hear with the inner ear.
With just these two developed senses, nobody can lie to
us. That is, we would never believe a lie since we would
know perfectly well that the person was not telling the
truth. It is amazing to listen to the endless lies that are
told day after day. People do not necessarily mean to be
untruthful. They have just forgotten what joy there is in
truth and what misery builds up over our lifetime if we
merely live in illusion constructed out of a continuous
pattern of untruthfulness.

It does not require much consideration to see that in
developing the higher senses we can be more of service
to others. Of course we must not expect results overnight.
It is also essential to keep thoroughly grounded as we
develop these gifts.

The trouble is that so many people, with their little
thinking minds fed only on comparisons, want immediate

results, and then, when they discover that this work demands tremendous effort and perseverance, they can develop a subtle form of resentment and even blame the teacher or the teachings for their lack of understanding of just the basic rules connected with the spiritual quest.

A true decision is made *outside of time* and so, when someone takes a step into the unknown, they cannot expect results to come about when they feel they deserve them. The search never stops for the true seeker. It is a question of moving on, step by step, day by day, month after month, watering the efforts that are made with conscious breathing and working in confidence and trust that, when the time is right, we will see at least some of the fruits of our labours.

There is no easy path to enlightenment as we are often taught to believe in the advertisements! There are surely some very quick methods to feed the ego until it grows so large that it blinds the seeing eye and locks the gates so tightly that it becomes a prisoner whose gaoler has lost the keys. For the spiritual seeker on the Road of Truth it is perseverance and good, solid, hard work and everyone should be warned about this before they set out on the journey. It would save so much disappointment and bitterness leading to a total lack of discrimination. The world of weekend workshops and seminars is filled with these instant enlightenment seekers, scarcely knowing which way to turn anymore. Make the senses your friends and develop the many other gifts that you are given, and true benefit will result in the end.

Let us explore one of the five normal senses and feel what it could be like to have all the senses equally refined. Imagine sitting by your window. What do you actually see? First of all, by being asked to do this, there is an immediate increase of available energy as we wake up. Perhaps there *is* something out there that we have not noticed before. A screen is pulled aside and life looks fresher and brighter.

There is also an immediate increase in this sensation when we remember the breath at the same time, but again we have to persevere. It is so easy for the mind to drift away into its usual conversation, thus wasting valuable energy which we need for this experiment. Bring the mind back to order by being awake to the breath. It will soon realise that it cannot go on playing games, even though it may well resist in the beginning.

In the next step, remember that it is you who is looking. Whatever you are seeing, no one else can see for you. Your view is unique to you. It cannot be anyone else's view because it is *your* view. Take responsibility for this knowledge. There is you and your view out there through the window.

Now be aware of the window and that you are looking through it. You are actually looking through a transparent solid piece of material, and, as we become awake to that, our view can take on another dimension. We can see the view more deeply because we have added something to the view, even if we cannot see it. In developing the sense we cannot presume anything at all. As we look out of our window we note that the view is different each moment. The changes make one smile!

Next be awake to the room *from* which you are viewing the outside world. Turn around in your chair and note the positioning of the furniture, the pictures on the wall, the flowers on the table, the books on the shelf. If you con- sider it, they are all part of the view. The room is behind us but with a little practice we can incorporate the room, and even the whole house, into our vision. We could then view the house and the surroundings all at once, and then one section at a time, as well as looking out of the window. The possibilities are boundless when we realise that we are not just two-or even three-dimensional beings, but rather we are multi-dimensional. Obviously our vision extends beyond the narrow confines of our everyday prison walls and there is a taste of greater freedom.

But we can go further. Still continuing with the breathing exercise, we now look through our eyes instead of from them. Again we have added another dimension, another possibility.

Now imagine that there is something or someone out there looking at us! We are part of their view. At precisely the moment we are looking we are being seen. Every single thing in the universe is subtly interconnected and so we are consciously fitting into the process of life. Somewhere between the in-breath and the out-breath, we can understand that what we are looking for is what is looking, and what we are seeing through the window needs and wants to be seen to bring it to life. 'Ah,' says God. 'Now I know one of my servants is doing a good job,' and He breathes out a sigh of relief which we hear coming in on the wind . . .

Listen, O dearly beloved!
I am the reality of the world, the centre of the
    circumference,
I am the parts and the whole.
I am the will established between Heaven and Earth,
I have created perception in you only in order to be the
    object of my perception.
If then you perceive me, you perceive yourself.
But you cannot perceive me through yourself.
It is through my eyes that you see me and see yourself,
Through your eyes you cannot see me.

Dearly beloved!
I have called you so often and you have not heard me.
I have shown myself to you so often and you have not
    seen me.
I have made myself fragrance so often and you have
    not smelled me,
Savorous food, and you have not tasted me.
Why can you not reach me through the object you
    touch,
Or breathe me through sweet perfumes?
Why do you not see me? Why do you not hear me?
Why? Why? Why?

(Ibn 'Arabi)

18

It Takes Time

'A healer is somebody who helps one towards wholeness.'

We are never given more pain than we can bear and, most certainly, real knowledge is painful to the false ego! Knowledge cuts through illusion like a hot knife through butter, and yet we are protected from more than we are able to understand. We can be given certain specific aspects of knowledge but if we are not empty enough, we cannot receive the essence of the teaching. Until what we have been given is distilled and digested within, we have really nothing to give away, and only by giving can we receive. That is our protection.

In this relative world it takes time to understand. It takes time to be emptied of illusions and it takes time for life to be brought to completion. We can even see the gates that need to be opened, but there are locks on both sides. First we have to find the key to open the lock from our side, and then it may take time for the gate to be opened from the other side. Here is a story which illustrates this teaching.

There once was a famous healer. Some people say that at one time he had been a doctor. Certainly he knew a great deal about both the physical and psychological aspects of the patients who visited him. After many years of work and, knowing that his time was limited, he decided to take on an apprentice so that his knowledge could be passed on to succeeding generations.

Many people applied for the job since he was so well known. He interviewed them all, making copious notes about their life-stories, and questioning them as to why they were applying. He cross-examined them concerning their motive and intention, who they had studied with before, and what countries they had visited. He was meticulous in his questioning, leaving no stone unturned. He was looking for just the right person, someone who was not veiled by their own self-importance, or contaminated by too many other people's opinions as to the true nature of healing. He told each of those who came that he would let them know within a month as to whom he had chosen. You can imagine the expectation!

One day, after many men and women had applied for the job, a young man came in. He was very shy, and almost apologetic in his request for an interview. Unlike the others, he had no real qualifications. He had not been to medical school or studied herbalism and other therapies, but he had been treated by the same healer when he was very young. His parents had brought him to the humble cottage with what the doctors had feared was an incurable disease, and he had recovered.

Somewhat nervously he told his story to the healer who, in this case, had ceased taking notes. In fact, he was smiling happily, occasionally giving a little chuckle as the young man's life story unfolded. 'Yes,' he said, in the middle of a sentence. 'You can have the job. There is no need to tell me more. When can you start?'

Of course the young man, whom we shall call Mike, was nonplussed. 'But, but . . .' he stammered. 'What about all the others? Surely they are better qualified than myself.'

'Mike,' replied the healer, 'they can have all the qualifications in the world, as far as I am concerned, but that does not mean to say that they will ever understand. I see you have that possibility for several reasons. Firstly, you came with no expectation. Expectation finally kills even hope. It eats up vital force and destroys the primal innocence of a true wish. The beauty of true belief, leading to living faith and pure trust, is stifled by the rotting garbage that grows from expectation, and then there is no chance of the necessary complete surrender which leads to Love. So that's the first reason I have chosen you.

'The second reason is that it must be the right time, for you have told me that you are free to work with me. You do not have any other commitments. You have come, as they say, "with both hands", and that gives me more chance to pass on what I have been given.'

'The third reason I have chosen you is because whatever training you have been given in the past has become part of your life. For instance, I noticed your manners. You stepped *over* the threshold of the doorway rather than on it. Who taught you that?'

'Oh, it was my father,' Mike replied. 'He used to say that whenever you go into someone's house, including your own, it is best to stop for a brief moment outside the door so that you can enter all in one piece, if you see what I mean. Then you are able to leave all that is not necessary outside the door before you go in. That is what he taught all of us and somehow or other I always remembered. When he was very old he reminded all of the family of the little lesson he had given to us as children, and said that before he died he was going to stay just long enough here to be able to step over the threshold into the next world. He said that he would tie up all his loose ends in this lifetime so that he wouldn't be any trouble to anyone, in this world or the next!'

The healer smiled. 'There are other reasons why I have accepted you, Mike, but they can wait. You might get all big-headed or something and then you would be deaf to the real teaching. So, you will start on the first day of next month. Bring clothes. You do not need books. I have plenty of them here, and I will pay you a minimum wage during your apprenticeship. There is a little studio room at the end of the garden and you can stay there.'

'But I thought I was to pay you,' Mike said, looking even more embarrassed. 'I have all my savings stacked away for just such an opportunity.'

'That is what they all think,' said the healer. 'But one day you will realise that it is my joy and pleasure to be able to teach, and so it is for me to pay you. Now, away with you, and I will have the room ready for you in three weeks time at the end of this month.'

The story of Mike's apprenticeship is really another book. Suffice it to say that he stayed with the healer for seven long years. Some of the years went quickly, and some seemed to drag on interminably. Sometimes he was sent away on short holidays 'to get the food of new impressions', he was told. Once he was asked to go to another country for several months, and just when he thought that his course of training was nearly over!

Initially Mike found everything very exciting, but that sensation soon faded and instead he felt great frustration. Nothing seemed to follow a logical course. Patients came and went; mostly they got better. They came with all manner of complaints from gallstones to cancer. One day the healer would lay the patients down on a bench and use his hands to work with magnetic healing. At other times he would make up herbal potions, which he concocted from a vast array of bottles at the back of his office. He never seemed to follow a set pattern, but rather each person was treated as the most special individual there was.

All during that period Mike was taught about conscious breathing and the subtle anatomy of the human being. He learned about the chakras and the channels through which the vital force moved. He learned so many different methods of healing that his notebooks were filled.

Towards the end of the seventh year, the two of them had become such close friends that I suppose they both avoided the moment when they would have to part, Mike to go out into the world to teach, and the healer to retire so that new knowledge would be given to his apprentice when the time was right.

One day, early in summer, there was a telephone call. Mike answered it, and the man at the other end of the line was obviously in great distress. He could scarcely speak, but Mike gathered that he had come all the way from the Middle East to see the healer. Apparently his fame had gone far and wide, and this man's teacher had sent him. He managed to explain that he was at the local railway station. Mike told the healer, and rushed off in the car to find him.

It was one of those special Scottish summer days. The first lambs were playing and the highlands were dusted with the colour of the heather. The nearest station was about ten miles away and it took a long time to get there. There were sheep on the road which had to be shooed off, and the early tourists sometimes blocked the tiny, narrow roads when they stopped to look at the view. It was hard for Mike to keep sufficient concentration during the drive. Obviously it was an important journey but those ten miles seemed like an eternity. 'Keep your intention before you at every step you take,' the healer had told him so many times. It was as though all the seven years training were crammed into those few miles of the Scottish highlands.

When he reached the station he found the visitor in very great distress. He was sitting, all huddled up on a bench. He had a battered old suitcase, and he had wrapped his overcoat so tightly around him that his face could scarcely be seen. He wore a lambskin hat pulled down over his ears. Mike wasted no time. He took him over to the car and said that the healer was expecting him. Then they started on the drive back. The man was wheezing and clutching his abdomen all the way in the car. His face was a greyish colour and Mike was wondering whether he should have taken him to the hospital instead. But that was fifteen miles the other way. He decided to press on. There were no words spoken.

Upon reaching the house, the man seemed worse than ever, but the healer was waiting, arms extended in greeting, and they all went back into the house. Mike was asked to make a special tea whilst the initial examination was taking place. It did not take long. The man had been diagnosed as having a serious internal disorder. His father had died of it and now his brother also had the same disease.

'I see,' said the healer. 'And you have come all this way to see me. Why do you think that I can help you?'

'Perhaps it is Kismet,' the man replied. 'It is a long way from Iran to Scotland, but still I had heard of you and was told that perhaps you could save my life.'

'I know of your condition,' said the healer. 'I feel we can help you very quickly. Mike, go to the back room, and on the top shelf you will see one of those glass jars marked with a red star. Bring that to me please.'

The back room was a mass of shelves, and it looked rather like one of those marvellous paintings of early pharmacies in Europe, jar after jar with coloured labels all written in incomprehensible Latin. Mike found the one with the red star and hastened back with it. The man was still clutching his abdomen and occasionally coughing. However, he seemed much calmer and there was a little colour back in his cheeks.

'Now I will have to see you every day for a week,' the healer said. 'We will find you a room in the local hotel. The food is good and it is very clean. In the meantime you are to take this.' Taking the glass jar, he opened the lid and inside there was some sort of a root. It looked rather like ginger, Mike thought. It was, in fact, the first time that he had seen inside that particular jar during the seven years he had been there.

The healer took a sharp penknife from his pocket and cut just three thin slices off the root. 'That is all you need,' he said. Handing the man the little pieces, he said that they were to be chewed carefully for the next ten minutes. He was to remember the breathing and be very still.

'What on earth did you give him?' Mike asked after they had left the room. The healer smiled and put his fingers to his lips. 'There are always secrets,' he said. 'This root is just the right one for his condition. Actually, I think he has got a parasite in the form of a large worm. I think this should deal with it!'

The man from the Middle East did stay and Mike would pick him up each day and bring him over to the healer's house for his three pieces of root. On the seventh day the little Scottish hotel rocked with an explosion which appeared to come from the bathroom! The man was indeed grateful for what had transpired. Immediately he called the healer. Mike picked him up in the car. His colour was rosy, his humour restored and he carried his overcoat over his arm. He was ready to say farewell. He was fine, he said, and the treatment had worked. It was the first time he had been out of pain for years. In fact, he was crying with gratitude.

'Thank you, thank you,' he said. 'Please, you take this.' From his suitcase he brought out a simple wooden box. Indeed for him it was a most generous gift. This was followed by much laughter and conversation. Later that day, before Mike was to drive him to the station where he would take the train to London and then back to Tehran, he asked if he could call his brother in Iran with the miraculous news. 'Of course,' said the healer. 'The telephone is yours.'

Neither Mike nor the healer could understand what was being said, but there was obviously great excitement in the air. The table was thumped many times to make some point or another and finally, when the telephone call was completed, the man came up and embraced them both, saying 'Allah, Allah' several times. The healer smiled again.

One week later there was another telephone call. Again it was a foreign voice from the railway station. It was the brother of the man who had recently left. Mike went to pick him up in the car and drove him to the healer's house. Again he made the tea whilst the examination was taking place. Eventually the healer and the visitor came out into the sitting room where Mike was waiting.

'I am very sorry,' the healer said, 'but I cannot help you. This is a far more difficult case than that of your brother. He should not have told you that I can cure everything. I shall have to meditate on this very deeply.'

The poor man was still clutching his abdomen in the same way as his brother did when he had arrived. He looked a picture of despair. 'You mean', he said, 'that you cannot help me like you helped my brother?' He actually got quite angry, standing up to make his point.

'Not now,' said the healer. 'I must pray and meditate on this, but I won't let you down. Now go and stay in the same hotel as your brother did. Eat the good food, walk in the hills, breathe the fine air, and come back in a week please.' The man agreed, as he had travelled half-way round the world to see if there was any cure for his terrible stomach-ache, and called most days to say that he was still at the hotel. On the seventh day he came back.

'My friend,' said the healer, 'I have prayed and prayed, meditated and meditated, and now I feel I have the answer. Mike, will you go to the back room and bring down that jar from the top shelf which is marked with a red star please.' Mike found the jar and brought it back. The healer sliced off three thin pieces of the root, told the man to chew it and to breathe consciously. That night another explosion rocked the little Scottish hotel and the man was healed.

Mike, after seven long years of his apprenticeship, was completely confused and exasperated. It was too much. The healer had surely manifested many miraculous healings during those years and often they could not be explained away by the logical mind. This time, however, it all seemed totally ridiculous. The first man had some sort of internal worm which, with the aid of the healer's medicine, took seven days to get rid of. Yet his brother, with an identical complaint, was sent away suffering for seven days before he was given exactly the same medicine, which only took a few hours to work rather than seven days.

In no uncertain terms, Mike expressed his feelings to the healer, who smiled more deeply than ever before. He knew now that his work was over. The apprentice had fulfilled his obligation and it was time for him to go. 'It's so simple,' he said, putting his arm round Mike's shoulders. 'But it took you seven years for me to be sent someone so that I could explain. God is the patient one, and yet He makes us impatient! It's not fair really. You see, the first man needed the three slices of root. His brother needed time and the three slices of root!

19

GATEWAYS

*'All the practices are to do with the balancing
within ourselves. In any real esoteric school,
there is a necessity to continue with practices.
It is essential as we go on the spiritual path to
keep the balance very carefully. When we get
into balance within, then it is possible we can be
open to the higher worlds without being swept
away in a gale of wind.'*

The chakras are situated along the spinal column. There
are other subtle centres, other gateways, but they remain
closed until we knock on them. With sufficient patience
and perseverance, they will then be opened from the
inside by the invisible gatekeepers. Everything takes time
in the relative world and this is for our own protection. If
the gates were suddenly to swing open, we might not be
sufficiently grounded to be able to accept the knowledge
that we would be given.

We proceed along life's journey step by step, always
doing our best to be awake to the moment, and that is
where breathing is again so important. Breathing is a total
experience, embracing all aspects of our being. It not only
keeps our lungs moving to provide the necessary oxygen
for our system, but it also connects us to the worlds
outside of us. By focusing our attention on certain parts
of the body, we can breathe into and through these areas,
activating them and bringing them to life. This is the key
we need to work on the locks of the gates. We can work
a little each day, knowing that although they have been
closed for so long, they will open again when the time is
right.

The practice I want to introduce at this time can be found in several esoteric traditions. The exact method may vary slightly, but the principle remains the same. Man is a many-dimensional creature, but it is seldom that everything is working in perfect balance. The object of any practice is surely balance and harmony, enabling us to live on many planes of consciousness at once.

Although there are obviously many gates that need to be opened, the six that we can activate in this exercise are connected to all the others through the subtle bodies. Working with them in the prescribed manner over an extended period of time can, and does, produce profound results. It is important to remember that although we do focus on certain areas of the physical body, this is only to give us direction. We are actually working with the subtle centres indeed.

Before you proceed with this practice, make a promise in essence that you will do this work without any expectation, and with no greed or ambition. This cannot be stressed strongly enough. No results will come from wrong attitude. It is only necessary to do the practice in love and for love. Attitude is very important and throughout this practice the correct attitude is one of gratitude. There is a certain inner sound that comes with this word. It is almost a sense of reverence and awe that we can even be allowed to be here and to be given some of the keys to unlock the gates.

Once you are settled and relaxed, in an upright chair with your back straight, begin the practice by establishing the rhythm of the breath. The rhythm is important. Breathe in to the count of seven, pause for one count, breathe out to the count of seven, pause for one count. The length of the breath and the speed of the rhythm is very personal and should be what feels comfortable for each individual. (See Addendum.) Watch the breath moving in and out and contemplate on the miracle of breathing. Just as life itself pervades every part of the universe, be aware of the breath interpenetrating every fibre of your being. You can stand up and walk in the open air, still remaining aware of the breathing. The practice can even be done standing up with your back pressed against the trunk of a favourite tree, but it is obviously essential not to let the mind wander. You will need all the energy of concentration you have. The eyes can be open or closed throughout the practice.

On the in-breath, breathe into the solar plexus. At the same time, through visualisation, you can consciously breathe in the energy from the earth and from all around you. Then, on the out-breath, imagine that you are breathing out from the centre of the chest, down through your arms and out through your hands. It is a beautiful sensation when this is done correctly, and of course the implications, even in human relationships, are very great indeed.

The first gateway is situated in the area of the physical spleen, that is, on the left side of the body just around the lower part of the rib-cage. Remember we are not just dealing with the physical body alone, which is the lowest level of vibration. There are many higher levels to which we can be consciously attuned with correct use of the breath.

Each of these centres has a different function, but working together they help us to come to a deeper sense of harmony with the whole universe. The first gateway provides a type of energy which is vitally necessary for our journey. That is why it is sometimes called 'Vital Force'. If we do not have sufficient circulation of this refined energy, then we are not necessarily able to fulfil our own personal destiny. Our concentration will be relatively poor and we can easily get diverted from our true aim. Paradoxically, without enough vital force, we do not feel that deep sense of peace that comes with everything moving together towards completion. This energy is not merely basic animal magnetic energy. It is a highly refined energy which is made available to us through inner work. It is refined through breath, sound and visualisation.

Now place your hands over the area of the spleen. If you are right-handed, place your right hand onto the body first, which is then covered by the left hand. If you are left-handed, it would be the other way around.

Breathe into the solar plexus as in the Mother's Breath*
and then breathe out, through your hands, into the area
of the spleen. Visualise pure light-energy flowing through
your hands and being received by that centre. At the same
time, whisper the sound of *Hū* (pronounced *Hoooo*) and
let that sound be carried deep into the spleen area to help
awaken this vital force. This should be done three times.

It is not necessary, or even advisable, to make this
practice last a long time. After three complete breaths in
the area of the spleen, move your hands carefully on to the
next centre, which is situated in the area just below the
rib-cage on the right-hand side. As you move your hands,
visualise this vital force being carried by them across the
body to the new area. Do not let your attention wander for
a single breath!

Just as the first centre had the two words *vital force*
associated with it, so each centre carries an idea. As we
activate the gateway above the liver, in the same way as
we did the first one, we contemplate on the word *wish*.
It is truly amazing how that one word can help lead us
towards our goal.

Can we imagine what it was like to really 'wish upon a
star' when the world was young and fresh? We all have a
primal innocence and enthusiasm with us that we knew
as little children, but so often it is covered up by the pain
we have suffered and the judgements we have made. Yet
the memory is still there and can be brought to life once
again.

What is it that we wish for? I don't mean merely
wishful thinking, such as dreaming of an expensive yacht
or beautiful home. What is our true wish? Is it freedom,
wonderful boundless freedom? Is it knowledge? What is
it? Ultimately our 'wish' is an entirely personal matter. It
is between us and our Creator, requiring only that we are
honest.

There is also the question of what we want for our
friends and family, what we would wish for the world.
The very word 'wish' is a gateway to higher worlds so that
impulses of a different order may enter our lives. We need
* See Addendum on *The Mother's Breath*.

to know what to wish for, and then we should not forget. It takes a lot of polishing to get the keys shiny enough to open the locks!

Having brought our hands from the first centre to the second centre, all the time aware of the vital force being transported with our breath and concentration, we again sound the *Hū* three times into this area. We are bringing the necessary energy into this centre to reawaken the wish in our hearts and, at the same time, we are coming closer to fulfilling God's wish for us. We can say 'Let Thy wish become my desire' and then there can be no duality or separation.

The next step is to move our hands, carefully, onto the third centre. This is situated in the area of the left breast on top of the physical heart. Again there is a key word to this centre. It is the word *hope*.

It is not easy to meditate on this word in a world that is so filled with suffering and pollution. I suspect there are many of us who, at one time or another, have almost given up hope for ourselves or the world. We pass a huddled figure on a freezing winter's night in New York or London, and we wonder what sort of hope, if any, that person has, and what hope there is in religious and political fanaticism which turns country against country, brother against brother. What hope is there for the millions dying of famine?

Yet there has to be hope. If we lose all hope, then what happens to God's hope for us? We can even forget that there *is* hope in the world, but it is we who have forgotten. There is hope in every heartbeat. Just as there is an inner sound of gratitude, so there is an inner sound lying within the word 'hope'. As we activate this centre, we pray we can remember what true hope is and, in doing so, we bring it forth into the present moment. We do sincerely hope for better things for everyone. Our voice is carried on the *Hū*, which, as in the first two centres, is sounded three times into this area.

Now, bringing our hands across the chest, we come to the fourth centre which is over the right breast. It is sometimes called 'the very secret place' and should not be forgotten. This time the key word is *belief*.

No matter how cynical we are, or how much we try to cover up true belief, it is always there in some form or another. These key words are powerful and it is sometimes useful to sit down with a notebook and write whatever arises when we meditate on them. What *do* we believe in? What would happen if we reawakened a living belief that has remained dormant for so long? Is it possible, through true belief, to come to such a state of conviction that we could leave this world with a credo that goes far beyond merely the concepts of the relative world, so that our children and our children's children may come to understand? It is a great challenge, but a wonderful one!

Without inner belief there can be no conviction in our own essential reality as part of the Whole. We fall into disappointment. Belief is not a complicated matter; it is belief in the ultimate goodness of all life. When we have conviction in this, knowing ourselves to be custodians of the planet, we will take the necessary steps to put ourselves in the stream of service. Love is pure energy and Love is not to be wasted.

Once again we sound the *Hū* three times, into this centre of 'belief'.

This exercise requires considerable practice so that we do not lose our attention for one split second as we move our hands from one area to another, at the same time visualising light/energy, contemplating the inner meaning and being awake to the rhythm of the breathing. Quiet persistence is the key to remember. Trying too hard will not help, but over a period of time we may be given some realisations from our work. Do not expect them necessarily to be given at the same time as we do the practice. As we all know, clear insight sometimes comes at very unusual times!

There are two more gateways to be opened. This does not mean to say that there are not more, but we can see these as the main ones to work with and then the others can follow. It would be incorrect to say that any one of the centres is more important than another, but it is useful to

know that the last two are also found in the same place as
two of the seven major chakras, i.e. the throat centre and
the one in the middle of the chest area.

The next step, then, is to move our hands from
the 'belief' centre to the throat centre. The throat centre
can be seen as having numerous jobs to do. All our food
and water is taken into the mouth and then passes down
through the physical throat, as does the air we breathe.
Our voice also comes from the throat. 'In the beginning
was the Word.' It is said that the first word was 'Be' and
then all became. The Divine command from the heart of
God was carried on the first manifested sound in the
universe, the sound of the *Hū*. It is here, in this area, that
we meditate on the idea of *pure surrender or abandonment*.
As we bring the vital force through our hands to activate
the throat centre, we open this gate so that the Higher
Worlds can work through us. There is a prayer that came
from the early Christian Fathers which I personally find
very helpful to repeat at this time:

The Prayer of Abandonment

Father, into Thy hands I abandon myself.
Do with me whatever You will and whatever
   You do
I will give thanks and remain always grateful.
Let Thy Will be done in me as in all of Thy
   creatures.

Into Thy hands I commend my spirit
I do so with all the love in my heart
For I love Thee, Lord,
And so long to give myself with a trust beyond all
   measure.

Amen.

'God needs man' and now we are prepared to surrender
ourselves for His Work on earth. Let Heaven come on

earth and may the earth turn into Heaven! The *Hū* is sounded again three times, into this centre, and perhaps we can begin to hear the Message that is carried to us, giving us the knowledge that is necessary to anchor love, the knowledge of ourselves.

The final part of the practice is as follows. Carefully bringing our hands from the throat centre to the centre of the chest, in gratefulness, we gently, and with full awareness, bow our head, visualising light in the centre of the chest. Whilst sounding the *Hū*, seven times for this last centre, we imagine a perfect red rose opening to the light under our hands. The contemplation is on the word *love*. We contemplate on God's love for us so that, in knowing we are loved, we can go out into the world, acting as messengers of His love. 'Love the Lord thy God and love thy neighbour as thyself.' The cycle is complete. Sitting quietly, we remain very still for a few minutes, our hands lowered to our knees. We can be sure that our prayers have been heard.

20

GUIDELINES

*'We are here to be committed unconditionally
to life. It is obviously only in the present moment
that any creative process can take place.'*

Of course there can never be an end to the process of self-discovery in this world, but guidelines can be given to help us along the way. That is what this book is all about. The discovery of our true nature is a wonderful adventure but can be fraught with pitfalls and dangers. Good teaching, coming from direct experience, is invaluable.

Every time some of the veils of illusion are stripped away from us, there is that moment of doubt. We may even fear that we are not on the right path. Yet we continue, always searching, living in the question as to the real reason and purpose of life on earth. Once we have entered the path of service there can be no turning back. It is as though we are in a long tunnel and there are so many other seekers behind us that all we can do is to forge on ahead, knowing there is light at the end, and when we see and experience this light, we will come to our own beginning for the first time. We understand that there is another sun behind the sun of our own universe, and then another sun, all leading to what is called 'the Light of Pure Intelligence'. The light behind the sun gives light to our sun, which in turn provides the means of life for our planet.

No one said that this 'life' was going to be easy. We experience moments of extreme doubt and fear, even despair, and then at other times, there is a real hope that is sensed in our hearts. However, these are just temporary states. We should not identify with them. If we are blessed with good advice and the correct tools to help us on this journey, we can undergo whatever is necessary to make completion possible. We can even hold the hands of those less fortunate than we are, passing on the knowledge and experience that we have been given. It is like a baton in a relay race. We surely all need each other, as we are needed by God.

The following guidelines are not written in any specific order or sequence. There are many ways that they can be used, but the most important thing is to realise that they *are* useful tools and obviously need a lot of practice so that they may become almost second nature to us. Take one guideline and work with it as a theme for a whole day, and then try two or more at once. Never presume the task is going to be easy but, at the same time, turn it into one of joy. Yet another challenge is offered to us!

•

1. *Be present at every breath; do not let your attention wander for the duration of a single breath.* This is a seemingly impossible task but if we have a clear aim and sufficient perseverance, little by little we do become more awake. We begin to remember ourselves more often and so can act spontaneously in different situations which require action as well as being still and quiet when that is what is needed. We start to grow in Knowledge. We say that God is the 'Only Knower', but there is no God but God!

Taking a conscious breath means being responsible for the moment itself. Again remember that breath is not limited by walls and concrete floors, nor high-rise office blocks and apartments. When we take a conscious breath, it does affect the whole, although we may never see the fruits of our labours. Time is both going out and returning on the Breath of Compassion. We all share the same air, but it is what we do with it that matters. Try to be conscious of the breath, not just for yourself, but for everyone else as well. Breathe in all that you need on the in-breath and send out light and loving thoughts to the world on the out-breath. The secret lies in between the breaths. Take every breath as though it is your last, for one day it will be.

●

2.   *Live in the question.* This is an art in itself. It is by living in the eternal question, as to the meaning of life, that real change can come about in our lives rather than just the apparency of change, when things just go on repeating themselves and no lessons are learned. We can begin to participate in conscious evolution as well as being part of organic evolution. Do not be afraid of asking the question; the answer needs to be found.

●

3.   *Watch each step that you take.* We are driving our car. It must not be allowed to run away with us. We wish for freedom, the freedom that lies in the knowledge of ourselves. Each day we can practise making the senses our friends. Remember, the sacred gateways wait to be opened. The cry for freedom is in everyone's hearts – freedom from unnecessary suffering, freedom from illusion, and freedom for our children and our children's children.

●

4.   *Always remember that we are travelling from a world of appearances to the true world of reality.* The spiritual journey is called returning to God. We are far away from our source and we want to go home to our true heritage. As it was said, 'I was a hidden treasure and I loved to be known, so I created the world that I might be known.' We do not need to look for Truth 'somewhere else', for the answer always lies right in the moment. The world was created for us as a stage for the greatest play of all to

be presented. That play is called Life. Time is the eternal attribute of God.

•

5.   *The key to will is gratefulness.* That is a tough guideline in a world in such a state as the one in which we find ourselves. However, it is surely true to say that if we are not grateful to be alive, then we are only partially conscious human beings. It is hard to be grateful when we are suffering, or mourning for a friend who has moved on. Yet, if we can truly wake up to be grateful in each moment and with each breath we take, then we do gain some pure will, which can then be seen to be a spark of the Divine Will. In Reality, there *is* only One Absolute Being by whose masquerade He both shows Himself in the world of form, at the same time as hiding Himself within it.

•

6.   *Practise the presence of God.* This means that we try to remember the Divine presence, both in our own hearts and in the hearts of others. We know that He – *Hū* – whatever name you give the Unnameable, is the Only Friend. By remembering this we help free the imprisoned God. We see the God in each other. Through recognition there is the beginning of freedom.

•

7.   *The sole purpose of Love is Beauty.* We try to do everything as beautifully as we can, whether we are working in the kitchen, painting a picture or building a house. We keep our lives in order, knowing of the interconnectedness of all life. If even the basement of our house is in a muddle, it has its effect on the other rooms. Order and cleanliness are entirely necessary on the spiritual journey. We try and live beautiful lives, and leave something

beautiful behind us when we go. No one can ever forget something of beauty, be it art, or poetry, music or dance. If we cannot paint or compose, or have no garden for people to feast their eyes upon, we can remember beauty and that is beautiful in itself for we can pass on the memory to others who are less fortunate than ourselves. The soul is beautiful and loves the beautiful.

●

8. *Struggle with all alien thoughts*. Pure thought can be seen as pure energy. What were we when we were a thought in the mind of God? In our separation from the Unity, most of our thinking merely comes from our loneliness, and various degrees of resentment, envy and pride. These types of thought are not useful. We do need to struggle with them. This struggle is an act of service both for ourselves and for others. Thought-forms are everywhere and unless we are awake, they stick to us like flies round a garbage can. They cannot be destroyed but they can be transformed. When we are awake to the breathing and the rhythm of the breath, always sending out light and loving kindness on the out-breath, little by little we can be free of thoughts that are useless to us, and have pure thought at our command.

●

9. *Learn how to forgive*. How many times are we told this! It is a hard task but absolutely vital in every way. There is a key here which can help us. Every word has a sound, an inner sound of meaning. There is a sound of forgiveness in the same way as there is a sound of gratefulness. Just as we say 'God is the Only Knower, the Only Provider, the Only Guide . . .', so He is the 'All-Forgiving'. We are His ears as well as His eyes, and the sound of forgiveness should ring in our ears all the time. We can find that sound for ourselves. It is there. We only have to listen very quietly

and carefully. We will be given that sound in our hearts and then we will never forget. It is judgement and blame that dull the ear of certainty.

●

10. *Seek out the true meaning of 'Judge not that ye be not judged'*. Judgement is based on past time, leaving patterns of rotting thought-forms which would be better put onto the compost heap. We cannot judge when we are truly awake for we can see the cause behind the cause and realise that the cause is indeed the effect of its own effect. Discrimination and judgement are very far away from each other.

●

11. *Patience is the key to courage* just as gratefulness is the key to will. We need all the gentle courage of he who can lie down with the lions. There is a great Sufi saying, 'There is no creation in the relative world; there is only the becoming of Being.' It takes patience to understand that! The 'Patient One' is also one of His Most Beautiful Names, and yet it is said in the Koran, 'And we created man impatient.'

●

12. Finally, *'Hold fast to the rope of God'*. 'God has no needs so give Him yours!' I remember there was one time when I could hardly sleep at all for many weeks. I went to my teacher, who looked at me and smiled. 'Good, Reshad. Now pray more for He likes to hear your voice.' God needs every prayer that He can get. Each time we are awake, remembering the breath and living in the question, we are making life as prayer itself and we are holding fast to the rope of God.

21

THE LIGHT BEHIND THE SUN – A VISUALISATION

'It is light that makes color visible.'
MEVLANA JELALLUDIN
RUMI

Sit quietly in a favourite place. Be very awake to the present moment. Sense your body and how and where it is sitting. Look around you, noticing whatever is there. Remember the senses we have talked about, and remember the interconnectedness of all life. If you are inside the house you could play some beautiful music.

Bring your attention to your breathing. Follow the breath in and out, like watching the tides on the ocean. Remember the quality of the breath and that we are all sharing the same element of air. Breathe in what you need so that you can breathe out light to the world. Do not try too hard to make this visualisation something special for yourself alone but rather make it an exercise in Beauty.

Now bring your attention to the rhythm and placing of the breath.* This puts us in harmony with the universal harmony. Listen to the sound of the *Hū* which is everywhere. It would be a good time to do the practice of the 'Gateways'.

•

Imagine that you are sitting on a beach by the ocean. It is that precious time before dawn. The first light is just creeping up onto the line of the horizon. The air is

*See Addendum on *The Mother's Breath*.

completely clear and fresh. Breathe in this air deeply. Fill yourself with its purity. Be purified.

There are a few stars still shining. Absorb the light of the heavens into your being. Feel the earth underneath where you are sitting. Breathe in the element of the earth. Listen to the sound of the ocean as you breathe in the element of water. All these are gifts of God. He wants us to take them, for this universe is made for us.

As you become more and more aware, sense the light moving over the horizon, getting brighter and brighter as the planet is turning towards the sun. Everything is so still and quiet. Now see the first rays reflected in the ocean. The stars go out one by one. The moon has veiled herself for another day.

Quite suddenly, as the sun cracks the barrier of night and day, it is possible to experience a different quality of sound. So soon the sun rises over the horizon! Feel its warmth on your chest and on your arms and face. Your whole body starts to warm as you sit there on the beach. The first birds are starting to wake. Everything begins to move as the sun gets higher and higher. It is the beginning of a new day.

Very carefully, follow the movement of the sun rising up in front of you, step by step, trying not to lose your attention for the duration of a single breath until it reaches its zenith directly above your head. It is noon. The world is at work.

Slowly, still awake to the rhythm of the breathing, sense the golden rays of the sun permeating every cell of your being. Bring the sun into the centre of your chest and let its rays of living gold pour out into the world. Now you *are* the centre of your own universe! No more are you breathing; you are being breathed.

Be very still.

There is a light from a greater sun giving light to your own sun. Open yourself to this light. Let it pour through the crown at the top of your head. This is the 'Light of Pure Intelligence', a light without colour as we know it. It is pure, unadulterated light, unfathomable to the normal human imagination, but always there, ready to

illuminate us. Through this light we can see the world as
a world of patterns, continuously unfolding from the one
still moment of creation.

Now we can be *in* the world and yet not *of* the world.
We are like a chalice made of the gold of the sun, able to
receive the Spirit from the Breath of His Compassion.

●

The exercise is over. Sit quietly for a while in the peace
of understanding. Become conscious of your physical
body once again. Remember the senses as friends and our
responsibility to be custodians of the planet. Look around
for a moment and see the world afresh. It is time to get on
with our daily lives.

22

DIE BEFORE YOU DIE

*'Asking a question from your heart can be
dangerous to the ego.'*

Once upon a time a seeker after Truth heard that there
was a fully realised man living in a faraway part of the
land. It was said that he was so far advanced in his
development that you had only to go and see him and
you, also, would come to full completion. The only thing
was that the man, who now had no more need to eat, was
lying in a coffin and was very protected by the villagers
where he lived. He had said that although he was alive,
he did not want to see everyone. 'Some just aren't ready,'
he said.

One seeker did find the village and, true to the story,
there was a coffin and lying in it was a man clad only in
white sheets. His eyes were closed and he was guarded
by four men, one at each corner of the coffin. The room
was cool and very quiet. The seeker entered. Just as he
approached the coffin a voice came from the man inside.
'Who is it?' he asked sharply. 'It is me,' said the seeker.
'Go away,' came the reply. 'There is no room for you and
me.'

The seeker was saddened. He had travelled all over
the world to find such a man. He went home to his wife
and children and prayed what to do next. 'Give him your
name,' said a voice from within his heart.

When he had gathered enough savings, he again went
to visit the village. The man was still there in his coffin.
He seemed to be breathing. All was well. 'Excuse me,' said
the seeker. 'I came a long way to see you last time but,
please forgive me, I forgot to give you my name and so you

sent me away.' He then very carefully and slowly gave his name. There was a movement in the coffin, a cough and a splutter. 'Go away. I told you there is no room for you and me.'

Devastated, the seeker left to return to his family once more. However, there was still this yearning within his heart. He prayed and meditated daily for several more years and then one day, just before going to his office, he understood. There *is* only One Absolute Being! Looking into his bank account he found there was enough money to get him back to the village for the third time. His wife was happy to see him go. Perhaps this time he would find the answer to his heart's desire.

The village was the same. There were still four men standing by the coffin. The enlightened one was as composed as ever in the coffin. This time the man almost ran up to him. 'Who the heck is it?' came the voice from the coffin. 'It is thou,' the seeker replied smiling. 'Ha!' said the shrouded figure, sitting up, eyes wide open and laughing. The guards took one look and fled. 'Good!' he said, stretching and climbing out. 'Now you get in. I'm bored.'

EPILOGUE

To die to the Truth is to die *in* Truth.

Life is nothing more or less than an experiment, made by God for us to come to understand. It is, was and will be an experiment. It's the Great Joke! We come into this life on the breath, and we go out on the breath. In between those two breaths *is* that great experiment. *Will* we love the Lord our God and will we love our neighbour as ourself? Who are we? If we do not know who we are, how can we love our neighbour as ourself? How can we know ourselves until, and unless, we sacrifice any concept we have of ourselves as separate from the One Divine Unity?

I leave you with this challenge.

Maui
Hawaii
11 NOVEMBER 1987

ADDENDUM

THE MOTHER'S BREATH

*'I can sow the seeds but you have to water
them with the breath.'*

The breathing practice that I teach is based upon a natural rhythm which is sometimes called 'the Mother's Breath'. This is the rhythm of 7–1–7–1–7. It is based on one of the great Cosmic Laws of the universe, the Law of Octaves. Much was written about this law in P. D. Ouspensky's book, In Search of the Miraculous.

The practice entails breathing in to a count of seven, pausing for one count, and then breathing out to the count of seven and pausing for one count. The rhythm is the most important thing and not the precise amount of time it takes to unfold in each individual. Each person is unique and we should find the pace that is most comfortable for us.

For a while the rhythm may be difficult. If our breath is not in harmony with the pulse of the universe, it will take practice in order to come back to what is our true heritage. The womb of the moment *pulsates* at a certain rhythm and this is understood through the practice of 7–1–7–1–7 breathing.

We have mostly presumed the breath. Although there are further dimensions to this practice, the first step is to watch the breath, in gratefulness to be alive in each moment. We follow the breath as it comes in through the nostrils and back out again, getting used to the rhythm of 7–1–7–1–7.

Now we can start work with the placing of the breath. Within us there is something which is sometimes called the 'cauldron', which can be likened to the

cauldron used in alchemy through which the transformation of the base metals are turned into gold. In this
practice we centre the cauldron in the solar plexus, and
we breathe into this area.

When we breathe in, we breathe in not only consciously but, in a sense, selfishly. By this I mean we
breathe in what we *need* for the necessary transformation
to take place. We can breathe in earth energy, magnetic
energy, colour, vibrations from the mineral kingdom, the
vegetable kingdom and so on. It is perfectly possible to
breathe in from all directions at once, into this central
point of the solar plexus. This should be a joyous experience, awakening wonder in the glory of being alive.

The next step has to do with out-breath. We breathe
in only to breathe out. What we have taken in on the
in-breath needs to be given to the waiting world on the
out-breath. And here, for the out-breath, we move our
attention from the solar plexus to the centre of the chest.
At the same time we visualise our breath radiating out
from that centre in all directions, manifesting as Light.
Each individual can add their own concepts of love and
goodwill towards all of God's creatures, from the planet to
Mankind Itself. I often give the analogy of the heart centre
being like a lighthouse for all the shipwrecked seekers in
the world.

Once again, the method of this practice is to breathe
in for the count of seven all that we need in the transformation process. On the pause of one count we raise our
attention from the solar plexus to the heart centre and
then we *radiate* out in the form of Light to the count of
seven, before pausing for one count. Then we repeat this
cycle over again.

Little by little this practice becomes perfectly 'normal'
and we find ourselves the right place and in the right time,
able to be more of service every day of our lives. The road
of the Sufi Path is called *the Way of Love, Compassion and
Service*. When this practice has been mastered, we can
feel a sense of true glorification in the privilege of what I
call 'Breathing Alive'. At last we can truly know that we
are loved, since God is love and 'there is no God but God'.

It is my most earnest wish that those of you who have come upon this message will do your best to make good use of the practice. I am sure that, as the years unfold, you will be given more details to add to this basic rhythm of the universe, the Mother's Breath, the pulsation of the womb of the moment.

May all be well!

Grace

For the food we eat
and
the water we drink,
For the wonders of the earth,
the sea and the sky,
For the sun and the rain, the moon and the stars,
For the early morning and the evening time,

For Thy love shown in
the Brotherhood of Man,

For all these blessings
and for so many more,
We thank Thee
Father.

Amen.